KT-408-542

RUSSELL BRAND

𝔄rticles of 𝔉aith

HarperCollins*Publishers*

Also by Russell Brand

My Booky Wook

Irons in the Fire

HarperCollins*Publishers*
77–85 Fulham Palace Road,
Hammersmith, London W6 8JB

www.harpercollins.co.uk

First published by HarperCollins*Publishers* 2008

1 3 5 7 9 10 8 6 4 2

© Russell Brand 2008

Russell Brand asserts the moral right to be
identified as the author of this work

A catalogue record of this book is
available from the British Library

ISBN 978-0-00-729881-5

Printed and bound in Great Britain by
Butler Tanner & Dennis, Frome, Somerset

All rights reserved. No part of this publication may be
reproduced, stored in a retrieval system, or transmitted,
in any form or by any means, electronic, mechanical,
photocopying, recording or otherwise, without the prior
written permission of the publishers.

Picture credits:
Art Streiber/AUGUST 18, 32; David Levene/Guardian News & Media 10, 15, 23,
64, 96, 146, 173, 193, 206, 212; Dean Chalkley 217

While every effort has been made to trace the owners of copyright material
reproduced herein and secure permissions, the publishers would like to apologise
for any omissions and will be pleased to incorporate missing acknowledgements in
any future edition of this book.

Mixed Sources
Product group from well-managed
forests and other controlled sources
www.fsc.org Cert no. SW-COC-1806
© 1996 Forest Stewardship Council
FSC

FSC is a non-profit international organisation established to promote the
responsible management of the world's forests. Products carrying the FSC
label are independently certified to assure consumers that they come
from forests that are managed to meet the social, economic and
ecological needs of present and future generations.

Find out more about HarperCollins and the environment at
www.harpercollins.co.uk/green

Contents

Introduction

I am writing this intro so that you feel validated in purchasing this compilation of columns. If I don't write it you might feel aggrieved that you've coughed up money (yuk! Who'd do that? You could only cough it up if you'd eaten it. I hate those people that eat coins and light bulbs and clock parts. Why don't they get a proper job? Like me for instance, I write a lovely column – and intros to column compilations – you won't catch me scoffing down change and chewing cogs then thrusting my coppery palm into your face for remuneration: 'If you wanted money you should of kept those pennies instead of gargling them down your whorish trachea' one might respond. I'm also against 'beards of bees' and, in fact, all records. I don't know how Guinness have snided their way into the world of records – it's none of their business, stick to booze, what's next – the Benson and Hedges encyclopaedia of maritime mysteries? The Skull Bandits almanac of porn? The Olympics can fuck off an' all – it's just the Paralympics for people who haven't suffered, it doesn't make sense. Running, jumping, swimming, triple jump, high jump. Don't they know there's a war on? Do they know it's Christmas? Timing things? Grow up. The only occasions on which my actions were timed were when my dad was tricking me into going to the newsagents. 'Go on, I'll time ya!' he'd say. Though by the time I'd return the competitive element had dissolved, replaced by fag-snatching indifference. Where's my medal? Where's my tickertape parade? I wasn't even allowed to keep the change. Luckily I nicked it anyway) only to read stuff you could've got for tuppence ha'penny with the *Guardian*, plus you'd've got all the ol' news in that an' all – not to mention those gorgeous tarts on page three and the weather. But with this book, you get all the articles – together at last, the cover picture, in which I am unadvisedly posing as Christ and interviews with famous football fans – providing I've had time to do them. What a bargain. I don't know why I'm trying to sell you this book; you've obviously already bought it. Unless it's a friend's copy or you're in a shop. If so, pop it in your jacket and walk out –

I don't care – I've already been paid plus I don't really do it for the money, I do it for the honour and my love of the art of intro writing. I could sit and write intros all day.

It just occurred to me that you might be reading this in the distant future, having chanced upon this in a second-hand book shop from the future. Should that be the case, get back on your hover-pod and watch the final glacier dwindle into naught and lament that you never knew the glory that was the 07–08 football season.

It was an incredible season, beset with drama and fused with romance. I love the game itself, of course, but these articles focus chiefly on my reaction to the phenomena of football culture – Sir Alex Ferguson, who doth abide and will ne'er relent, like a face carved into the edifice of the national game as though it were Mount Rushmore; Kevin Keegan, who in the past brought Newcastle so close to success but now has the air of a Sunday league dad hollering 'go on my son – they don't like it up 'em' from the touchline; Avram Grant, poor unlovable Avram whose legacy is as murky and as difficult to judge as the dental blur that resides betwixt his lips; Ronaldo, a man allegedly labelled a slave by that flippant nit Sepp Blatter – a tag he did too little to shed ('Yeah, I am like a slave – I remember that episode of *Roots* where Kunta Kinte, reclining in silver hot pants, got noshed off on a yacht by a never-ending procession of gorgeous floosies – no wonder he was peeved.'). Ronaldo has remained at United, wisely allowing his free will to be coaxed into acquiescence by the endlessly successful Fergie. I'm sure he'll be a better man for it but how can he top last season?

Then of course there's my beloved Hammers, for whom it was a relatively uneventful year, which typically means that the subsequent season will see Upton Park burned to the ground or Lionel Messi join the club – West Ham cannot be mediocre with any degree of consistency, they are defined by volatility. Or should I say 'we' for Paulo Di Canio himself, one of the club's most beloved anti-heroes, referred to the institution of West Ham as 'you' while addressing 'me'. A team he played for for over four years and yet he grammatically acknowledged the strength of my allegiance. This is where the game's power lies. When abroad, if I see someone in the shirt of a British football team, even Tottenham, after ascertaining that they're not dangerously drunk, I will make eye contact and talk. About football. It gives us a common language. We recognise that whether you're hollering for Hull City to stay up or for Manchester United to gobble up another cup, what you're actually doing is submerging your identity as an individual into a whole that is common to us all. Separation is an illusion and in a game that is built around opposition we discover that ultimately we are all one.

1

This year I'll ride the snake like a soccer shaman

Today I am going to watch West Ham vs Man City for the first game of the new calendar. The season's commencement feels all fresh, lovely and new. We've rinsed away the horror and regret of last season; I suppose that's another of the sublime delights entailed within the game – a terminable, manageable existence within defined parameters. Regardless of how spectacular or drab your term has been it'll all begin again next August. That's comforting. Better than actual life where if you hijack a bus and drive it into an old folks' home yawping slogans and hurling fireworks the consequences will haunt you to your grave.

I shall make my way to Upton Park all virginal and brimming with innocent expectation with a couple of chums, perhaps singing 'three little maids from school are we' from the *Mikado*. Noel Gallagher will be there in his capacity as a City fan elevating further the jeopardy for this already thrilling encounter as football kindly provides a context for good-natured banter and playful threats – again within defined parameters.

The close season, or anti–season – a kind of negative un-time that exists only in relation to the Platonic, pure season – has been a fiscal torrent with cash flooding the Premiership and now buoyant corpses bloated with expectation bob towards the first whistle.

'I shall make my way to Upton Park all virginal and brimming with innocent expectation'

There has been much condemnation of the way in which the influx of money has poisoned the game and it's difficult to dispute that recent events have tarnished football's romance. But the effects of rampant capitalism are not confined to peculiar transfers and boardroom espionage – it's ballsing up the entire planet. I saw in a red top that cocaine was found in the lavvies at 25 per cent of Premiership grounds, implying that the clubs are somehow culpable. People take cocaine; people go to football, that is all that's been proven in that barmy cistern survey. Similarly the whole world is governed by an ideology that demands that the acquisition of money must subjugate all else: morality, spirituality and good old-fashioned sexiness are secondary to commerce, and this cannot be blamed on Carlos Tevez, Malcolm Glazer or even Thaksin Shinawatra, although he might've been closer to the nub of the problem in his last job.

When caught up in the magic of live football it's easy to believe that the power of the crowd is what ultimately matters; the inherent unity feels like socialism but each of the screaming 34,000 has been taxed on entry and however loud they may sound their voices are seldom heard. It is apparently futile to resist progress although tiny victories are occasionally achieved: disenchanted Manchester United fans have established FC United, a collectively financed club that truly belongs to its supporters. Presumably, though, were the club to clamber through the multitude of leagues to penetrate the national consciousness and challenge for trinkets the inevitable tide would also consume this idealistic vessel.

Adrian Johnson

Myself, I get all caught up in the rhubarb, I'm intrigued by escalating transfer fees and bonkers wages, I enjoy the soap opera. How can United fail to win the title this year? They've assembled a terrifying gang of world-class players, and quaint idealism aside I'm tantalised by the prospect of seeing Tevez hook up with Rooney. Chelsea's current injury problems may impair them early on but that Malouda bloke looked good in the Community Shield and they know how to scrap. I'd like Liverpool to do well – Torres is a handsome devil and I'm sure he'll cause all sorts of bother. Arsenal have a stability which oughtn't to be underestimated and were coping without Henry for the majority of last season. And I suppose we'll all be interested to see what Spurs do with their panoply of strikers.

There's been more diverse transfer activity than in recent memory but I'll still be surprised if the top four in May ain't the typical blend of red and blue. Newcastle, Villa, Pompey, Blackburn, West Ham and Sunderland will be shuffling around the Uefa places and I think Reading, Bolton and Wigan might be auditioning for the fizzy pop league.

Apart from the obvious top four element I'll be interested to see how those predictions pan out because I have an unscientific mind fuelled chiefly by emotion and whimsy. I shall be utterly agog if come next August the above paragraph doesn't appear to be the result of a drunken, myopic pianist being deceived that my keyboard is a futuristic Steinway and told to 'just go nuts'.

I shall enjoy this year's football; I'll ride the snake, like Jim Morrison as a soccer-ball shaman. I'm not going to focus on the incremental erosion of the essence of the beautiful game because it is symptomatic of a much larger problem. I'd like to suggest that we enjoy the football then come late May, in the unseason, instead of watching the to-ing and fro-ing and the 'I'd rather not going' we unite under one glorious banner, march down Whitehall and kick off a proper revolution.

2

A pitch-perfect
ending to a sadly
familiar song

Sven-Goran Eriksson's Manchester City commanded play at Upton Park last week with such assurance and grace that far from seeming a hastily assembled squad of mercenaries from around this dirty little circle we call 'world', they appeared to be afloat in a transcendental love affair with each other and the randy boffin who compiled them.

Flicks and dummies, winks and one-twos, it had the gleeful complicity of a well-administrated orgy at a hostel for handsome backpackers. What's a bit annoying from the perspective of an Englishman is that now Sven can utter the damnation that secretly we all suspected to be true; he can manage perfectly well once liberated from the tiresome obligation to select only sons of Albion. As he said himself: 'There was no Elano to pick for England.' Blast.

Rolando Bianchi, who got City's first, ran directly over to the dugout to give Sven a cuddle, publicly consummating the Manchester love right in front of the embarrassed West Ham fans. We didn't know where to look; most people opted to rest their disillusioned peepers 'pon Dean Ashton, warming up on the sidelines for most of the match with a peculiarly erotic, slow-motion, sexy karate-robot dance.

For me the opening day of the season was an oscillating mind waltz of conflicting emotions. The Irons were pretty shoddy, disorganised in midfield, lacking in imagination up front and a nerve-jangling ballet of tipsy confusion is what passed for a defence. Only Robert Green in goal and Mark Noble looked comfortable.

The ignominy was exacerbated by the prior knowledge of an after-match meeting with Noel Gallagher in Christian Dailly's box. Most people are aware that the Gallagher brothers are arrogant as a default setting, a feat they performed whilst supporting an unreliable and often risible football team. Well let me tell you that all the swagger and bluster we endured as discs went platinum and Brits were won were as nought compared to the gloating, showboating, puffed-up rhubarb I had to silently tolerate in a senior player's box after Saturday's misdemeanour.

I'd rather hoped that it would be me bragging and strutting, perhaps whilst chuffing on a cigar, consoling a tearful Noel that the season is yet young and that he'd made some jolly good records. Instead me, my dad, my mate Jack and Robin the hippy black cab driver (there's an anomaly – if you leap into his carriage unawares it's like a magical mystery tour as he recites poems and demands a more lax immigration policy) moped about, overjoyed to be amongst adored West Ham players (James Collins was also there like a big, twinkly beefcake) but irked by the unanticipated defeat.

'Strolling on to the eternity lawn at the Boleyn makes my brain stop gurgling and my eyes do crying'

Then something magical happened. Dailly, who was about to take his adorable trio of wee Daillys to have a kick-about on the pitch, turned to us and said 'Do youse wanna come down an' all?' None of us have ever been on the pitch at Upton Park. I'm not a man who is much at ease in any arena designed for physical activity but to walk on to the turf of the team you've supported all your life, were deigned to support, even before birth, is like climbing into the telly or being given the keys to Wonka's chocolate factory and being told, 'Here, just take it, I'm dispensing with all these bonkers tests and riddles – too many children have died. Poor, dear Augustus Gloop.'

Although, retrospectively, running a chocolate factory is probably a pain in the arse, whereas strolling on to the eternity lawn at the Boleyn makes my brain stop gurgling and my eyes do crying. On the way we sneakily looked into the away dressing room – which looked like it had played host to a tea party for giant toddlers. There were bottles and grass and fruit scattered about the room like Jackson Pollock working in litter. You could still feel the echo of the departed, triumphant City players, you could envisage them congaing out behind Sven, covered in victory and streamers.

Then we were in the tunnel. A mural of West Ham legends adorned the walls; Brooking, Dicks, Moore, Devonshire, lit by the glare from the end of the tunnel, the light reflecting green. A few more tentative steps with the opening notes of Bubbles played by a phantom orchestra (or possibly covers band) and there it was, Upton Park, scene of misery and celebration, venue for rites of passage for hundreds of thousands of men, barely an hour before fizzing with hope, then saturated in defeat, now silent, empty, and Bagpuss was just a soppy ol' stuffed cat . . .

But there amidst the burgeoning nothing, chatting to Dailly, all normal, stood Dean Ashton, radiant with health, which is odd 'cos he's a few weeks off full fitness. My mate Jack stuck out a hand. 'All right, Deano.' Dean being, in reality, a bloke rather than the subject of an unrelenting sonnet rolling around the mouths of 30,000 even before he'd kicked a ball, simply replied: 'All right.' I scuttled over like a ninny and accosted Dean. I don't remember what I said but it can't have been great because I felt the necessity to impersonate Dean's warm-up dance routine which, looking back, strikes me as an act of desperation.

Dean laughed. As did the few people remaining in the ground, mostly in the directors' boxes. Then I met Alan Taylor, scorer of two Hammers goals in the 1975 FA Cup final, while my dad, Jack and Robin the hippy cabby kicked a ball around the Bobby Moore Stand end of the pitch with Christian Dailly's kids. 'Come on Russell, join in,' someone shouted. I declined; I could only have tarnished perfection.

David Humphries

'Wembley and Germany are typically powerful sirens to summon my slumbering jingoism. Not this time'

3

A pledge is not
enough to make
England shine

You know them pledges we make when England are knocked out of major tournaments on penalties? Typically the pledge will be formed along the lines of: 'England, you have betrayed us and shamed us. Worse than that, you have given us momentary hope, and hope is so much harder to withstand than despair, thus I shall never more be inveigled into caring about your results or supping the toxic broth of brouhaha that surrounds the carnival of fools we call our national team.'

'If it was up to me I'd put chimps in the team, and ballroom dancers'

'Tis a long and solemn oath. That's usually how it is for me; then the tournament continues without England, all pale and ghostly, and I'm left to ponder what I do with my life, drifting listlessly, unable to feel, involving myself in any senseless bagatelle just to try and stir some emotion. Then, like a tragically willing victim of spousal abuse, I find myself lured back into the tempest by the gorgeous oaf that is patriotism and the incessant promise that they've changed.

Well, I think that on Wednesday I might've broken the cycle. I know it was a friendly but it was at Wembley and against Germany – two powerful sirens that are typically sufficient to summon my slumbering jingoism. Not this time.

I just went out and got on with my life. 'Alan Smith might play', I heard echoing through ol' Jung's collective brain box. I continued with my chores. 'Joe Cole will be given a more creative role' – I remained undeterred. 'Micah Richards is gonna get his willy out' – I was curious but did not seek out a Dixons window in which to confirm the rumour.

Everyone's quite rightly excited by Richards but am I alone in detecting homoerotic undertones in the relentless drooling about his athleticism and his 'leap'? 'Ooh, what a leap,' pundits say, struggling to stifle a stiffy; 'I've never seen a leap like it'; 'I wish he'd leap into my parlour, then leap on to my bunk, then leap about on my tummy till I cry guilty tears about my bastard marriage vows.' That's what they say, these pundits. They say it with their eyes.

Micah 'The Leap' Richards is the most encouraging thing about England but I was not seduced into watching the game because I still feel a bit despondent about international football. I think this is because of the following:

1. Steve McClaren. I believe him to be a bit of an appeaser – 'You want Beckham back? Have Beckham back.' He seems to make reactionary decisions and as much as we might think we can manage England, we can't and shouldn't be allowed to. 'Don't listen to me,' I feel like saying, 'I'm whimsical, capricious, vindictive and jealous. I make stupid decisions.' If it was up to me I'd put chimps in the team, and ballroom dancers. It'd be ridiculous, but fortunately I have no power.

2. The team is going backwards through time with McClaren like an autistic archaeologist digging up veterans and former heroes who can only sully their good names. David James? Sol Campbell? Why not reinstate Bobby Charlton and get him to play a quick half. In fact get the entire pub team of legends from that beer advert and give them a go.

3. Sometimes I get depressed but it passes and I only think it's really bad when I think, 'What would make me happy?' and I can't think of anything. That's how England make me feel now. What would make it work? David Bentley? Aaron Lennon? Robert Green? There was a time when we'd clamour, that's right clamour, to have someone in the team: 'Pick Rooney' – 'But he's only 12'– 'PICK HIM'. Or, 'Take Gazza' – 'He's drunk' – 'TAKE HIM'. Now at the first sign of a clamour we're obeyed, it takes all the fun out of the clamouring. Having said that, PICK ROBERT GREEN.

Those are my three reasons. I dare say once the games become competitive I may feel a tingle but Premier League football hoovers up loyalty like a junkie anteater so it'll never again be as painful as Italia 90 or Euro 96 or that kick in the nuts last summer. I shall enjoy international football perched like a connoisseur on a barstool of snooty indifference. And you can take that pledge right down to the ol' pledge bank.

Dark lore of Dyer
and the Hammers'
hex

4

I suppose, were I able to trade in some cosmic stock exchange, I would relinquish West Ham's passage into the third round of the League Cup in order to preserve Kieron Dyer's lower right leg. As Alan Curbishley said after the win against Bristol Rovers: 'Now the result seems immaterial.'

It's difficult to celebrate victory having seen Dyer suffer one of those wince-inducing injuries where the leg visibly contorts within the sock and it seems impossible to imagine it ever healing. It will, of course, in time, six months or so, but that's the bulk of the season without him and he looked sharp and fast against Wigan last Saturday.

I feel dead sorry for him, in a hospital somewhere hurting. Obviously I don't know what it's like to be a professional athlete but it must engender a particular insecurity to be dependent on your body in such a palpably direct manner. Whenever I suffer great physical pain or even mild discomfort it immediately resets my psychology to neutral. Say if I feel all sad and self-indulgent then get stung by a wasp, my misery feels quite abstract and I long just to be in spiritual pain once more – 'Damn you tiny assassin, all clad in yellow and black, how I crave my former innocence where melancholy was my only trial.'

'What?! Arsenal away in the fourth round? Damn you, Lucifer. Why have you forsaken me, Lord?'

It's terrible news for West Ham, and Curbishley implied there might be a jinx as so many of the players he's bought in have suffered injury. It is bloody unfortunate, but a curse? After last season's controversy plenty have grudges, not least in the city of steel. Could former Blades boss Neil Warnock be poised in a circle of stone, stinking of chicken's blood, spewing white-eyed incantations and clutching a buckled dolly of Julien Faubert?

There appears to be a troubling tendency among under-pressure Premiership managers to jab accusatory digits in the direction of the dark arts – Martin Jol cited 'black magic' as the reason Spurs didn't get a penalty at Old Trafford at the weekend. Perhaps Tottenham did deserve something from a tie in which United were less than brilliant and they doubtless had chances but the resulting home win surely owes more to Nani's right foot and Wes Brown's chest/upper arm than Aleister Crowley's necromancy.

Perhaps this is a further indication that top-flight managers are under too much pressure, when in our secular age they crumble into medieval beliefs whenever luck goes against them – 'What?! Arsenal away in the fourth round? Damn you, Lucifer. Why have you forsaken me, Lord?' However, the injury crisis at Upton Park, if not the work of Beelzebub, is critical: Dean Ashton, Scott Parker, Dyer, Faubert, Freddie Ljungberg and both Lucas Neill and Matthew Upson joined the afflicted minutes after they signed. The only solution available to the club is to keep signing more

Matt Johnstone

players, an approach I believe was pioneered by Stalin in his gruelling fixture against Hitler on the Eastern Front.

His mentality was, as I understand, 'Right, loads of Germans are dying, loads of Russians are dying and we're both going to continue to pour young men into this battle until it's resolved, but as Russia has a larger stack of human chips we can carry on playing beyond the point of German exhaustion. I feel the hand of history, not on my shoulder but cheekily goosing me out of respect.'

Let's hurl more millionaire footballers onto this bonfire of the lame; why wait till they arrive at West Ham? Just give Eidur Gudjohnsen a sack of money then smash him in the balls with a pool cue. Let's buy a wing at Whitechapel hospital and send an army of thugs with chequebooks and chainsaws on a tour round Europe to assemble a hobbling chorus of convalescents. I wish Dyer a speedy recovery. It's a shame, and as an offer of appeasement to the angry football gods I shall sacrifice the next virgin I meet on Green Street. It could take a while.

5

Never mind Israel,
I've been beaten
by Bohemia

I am writing this at the Chelsea Hotel in New York, where Arthur Miller wrote *A View from the Bridge*, where Sid Vicious killed Nancy Spungen and where Leonard Cohen received 'head on an unmade bed' from Janis Joplin. As is the case with most hotels trading on history, it's a bloody dump.

When I phoned reception in the dead of night to ask for water, water, I was told: 'There's a deli across the street.' In Maslow's hierarchy of needs water is right there with shelter and excretion at the pyramid's foundation; they may as well dispense with the toilet and the building; they could just have a bellhop stood in the street charging you $200 a night for crapping in the gutter and snuggling up with Oscar the Grouch. Comprised neatly in this scenario is the perennial issue of the romantic versus the pragmatic – you don't stay at the Chelsea for room service, you stay because you're renting a little counter-cultural history for the night.

'Rio said not qualifying is "unthinkable" but that just sounds like Chris Eubank describing the *Titanic*'

Today England face Israel at fortress Wembley, God help us. A draw against Brazil, defeat against Germany – it's not exactly impenetrable. Steven Gerrard has his own romance v pragmatism choice to make – does he play with a fractured toe, knowing his significance and skill are vital to Blighty, or does he heed the advice of his club and convalesce?

It seems that Stevie will play, which worries me for a couple of reasons. I hope no one treads on his foot in the game of football he is playing against Israel's national football team on a football pitch. Also it is difficult not to be concerned about the state of our squad when sickbeds have to be trundled to stadiums like wheelbarrows and tipped on to the field so we can scrabble together 11 men.

In addition to Steve McClaren's grave-robbing selection policy – this week Emile Heskey, next week Dixie Dean – it leaves me thinking that not qualifying is a realistic possibility. Romantically, I think, 'No, England shall qualify, 'tis our destiny. None shall pass.' But bloody hell it don't look good. Rio Ferdinand said that not qualifying is 'unthinkable' but that just sounds like Chris Eubank describing the *Titanic*. It is thinkable, too bloody thinkable, I'm thinking about it right now in Yanksville, Americee, where in '94 a World Cup took place in which there was nobody speaking proper English and Alexi Lalas was just a Hanna-Barbera flesh sketch, a living Shaggy, not yet the manager of another resurrected McLazarus selection.

It's awful when England don't qualify; I'd rather watch every woman I've ever loved drunkenly fellating handsome idiots at a bus depot than sit through another USA '94. Actually the bus depot thing could be quite sexy, inducing a masturbatory experience that flits between jealousy and intense excitement, where one cries, despite oneself, during the act of onanism. I believe it's popularly known as a 'cr-ank'. But I'll be damned if I'm going to crank my way through Euro 2008. I'm older now and more dignified.

How are we to avoid this phantom of a nation lost in sexual flagellation – which would be an awful, Catholic, Marvin Gaye anthem: 'In this

Neil Fox

situation I need, sexual flagellation, get up, get up, get up, let's cry-wank tonight'? It'll never catch on, so how do we avoid it? Where do we look for salvation? Dear, hobbling Stevie Gerrard? Confidence junky Emile Heskey? Joe Cole? Possibly, but he's not starting for Chelsea and I don't think he's ever recovered from Glenn Roeder's barmy decision to make him put on two stone – why did he do it? He might as well've bulked up Darcy Bussell or Harry Potter.

I don't know if I'll be able to watch the qualifying matches as I'm all caught up making a documentary about Jack Kerouac and *On the Road* for the BBC and I've got more chance of discovering the essence of being that the Beats quested after than a telly showing soccer-ball – even in the Beckham era.

Good luck England. I reserve the right to flood these pages with hyperbole if we beat Israel and Russia, and begin a campaign for McClaren's knighthood. Such is the nature of football. Now for a spot of breakfast at the Chelsea, which will most likely be a lampshade smeared in peanut butter, by me with a room key. No wonder Sid killed Nancy – he was probably hungry and had a delirious vision of her as a hamburger. Arthur Miller was probably bored into writing that play and I bet Leonard and Janis's bed was unmade when they arrived.

Repent, for the
kingdom of Steve is
at hand

The one thing that could perhaps redeem the column I wrote seven, vast days ago; immense days, days with the limitless, intimidating scale of the expansive Kansas plains that I've been crossing this past week is that, at its close, having spent 800 words fear-mongering, I did offer, with rare perspicacity, the sentence: 'I reserve the right to flood these pages with hyperbole if England win both matches.' Well England did win both matches but hyperbole is not what I'm going to offer, no, I think more appropriate would be contrition. I feel contrite at having referred to the team's key player in those games, Emile Heskey, as a 'confidence junky'. So what if strong, committed, unselfish, skilful Emile sometimes requires what Ron Atkinson (note: this stereotyping refers to pre-racist Ron, when he was just a bejewelled vending machine for clichés) would doubtless describe as 'an arm round him' once in a while.

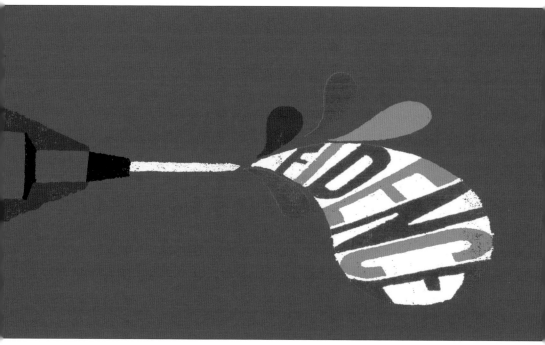

Adrian Johnson

I think that's rather lovely. In this age where the modern footballer is regarded as a brash millionaire floozies-harvester, players like Emile, and indeed Shaun Wright-Phillips, occasionally suffer from self-doubt and need assurance from their manager if they are to perform to their potential. Unhelpful then to reduce Heskey to a man who uses esteem like a drug and sees his coach as the pusher, hence 'confidence junky'. Sorry.

Also in my doom-laden scribbling I conjectured with grisly portent that Steven Gerrard would end up in a wheelchair as a result of fierce Mossad attacks or assaults from ex-KGB but, I now accept, he seems to be fine. Again, I'm sorry.

Then dear, triumphant, indefatigable Steve McClaren or 'McLazarus', as I dubbed him due to his tendency to resurrect dead or at least departed players, a tendency which I now realise marks him out as brave and willing to take risks rather than being a victim to the whims of an all-too-fickle press, of which I must now stand as the worst example. Also 'McLazarus' doesn't quite work because the biblical character Lazarus, upon whom my cruel, cheap pun was based, was resurrected by Christ and did not resurrect anyone himself, so I've offended theologians as well as the great tactician McClaren.

I've had scores of complaints from theologians but I'm less concerned about insulting a group who have forgiveness as one of their core tenets than I am noble McClaren who is as wise and gracious as Christ. I'm so very sorry.

'When I left, McClaren picked his teams like a drunk shuffling bags in a trolley. Now he is indispensable'

I did also say that Alexi Lalas looks like a live action version of the *Scooby Doo* character Shaggy. I stand by that. Thank God I didn't have time to express my ill-informed views on Michael Owen who I would've probably dismissed as 'finished' or 'a bastard' but would now like to celebrate as a great servant of the game who will doubtless surpass Bobby Charlton's 49 goals during the qualifying phase of this tournament, a tournament that last week I revealed grave doubts that we'd be attending beyond this formative stage but now firmly believe we'll win.

Furthermore I cast aspersions on Owen's assertion that Wembley would become a fortress, claiming it was as impenetrable as Nancy Spungen's jugular. I was writing the piece in the Chelsea Hotel and it seemed a fitting simile as it was there that Sid Vicious for once lived up to his name and murdered her. The line was cut from the published article on grounds of taste – I only wish the censor's pen had removed the relentless, pulsating pessimism which seeped through the column staining the page the way Nancy's blood did the tarnished floorboards of my hotel room.

Tentatively, let me say this: West Ham were tumbling towards the Championship last season with such fervour and pace that one could be forgiven for thinking that the players were sexually aroused by the prospect of poor stadiums, then I went to Hawaii to work and they immediately became a squad of well-drilled, committed heroes winning eight of their last nine fixtures.

When I left the country 10 days ago England were playing like a bunch of berks and McClaren picked his sides like a homeless drunk shuffling bags in a trolley. He is now indispensable and Gareth Barry is the new Bryan Robson. I said if England won both games I'd campaign for the manager to be knighted; I now demand that Her Majesty kicks Phil right out of the royal sex-pit and instates Steve as her lover and the new King of England. I'd also like her to sit beside him on the bench and squeeze his thigh and coo when things go well.

Well done England and sorry for last week's column. Prudently, I've read this week's column back and I've written nothing that could offend anyone, what a relief. Finally, huge congratulations to our dear brothers north of the border. I should probably stay in America for football's sake.

Chelsea too
small for these
two randy stags

Jetlagged and delirious, I'm trying to make sense of the events that adorn the front and back pages of the English newspapers. José Mourinho and Chelsea have parted company 'by mutual consent' due to a 'breakdown in their relationship'. This doesn't seem to me to be the typical language of the boardroom but the brittle nomenclature of damaged emotions. When I recall the numerous occasions on which I've been, in my case deservedly, sacked, my incensed employers seldom said things like 'It's not you – it's me' or 'I just feel we should spend some time apart.' It was usually 'Get out you thief' or 'You smell of gin.'

I'm not suggesting that Mourinho and Roman Abramovich were having a big, saucy, gay love affair that has ended in recrimination and unfulfilled potential but the fact that it would be impossible to allocate who would be passive and who the aggressor in such a tryst is perhaps central to this saga. Whilst I acknowledge that most homosexuals chuckle at the antiquated, heterosexual assumption that gay relationships have a 'man' and 'wife' dynamic, partnerships the world over are defined by status, and the inability of these powerful men to find professional harmony, to me, resembles two randy stags, nostrils flared, bristling, with angry erections, locking horns over which one is going to bite on a branch and be Bambi's mummy.

'Mourinho provoked a kind of neutered lust. I enjoyed his manipulative interviews and eccentric outbursts'

Ultimately Chelsea are Abramovich's club and there could be only one winner but as a result we, the English nation, the Premier League and the media, have lost an intriguing and charismatic figure.

Like most people I became aware of Mourinho when he darted down the touchline arms aloft in *that* coat, at Old Trafford, having engineered

Porto's victory over United. 'What a twit,' I remember thinking. The fact that the coat became independently famous is a testimony to the unique place he attained in the firmament of top-flight bosses. What other garments have secured such cachet? Brian Clough's green sweatshirt? Arsène Wenger's specs? Fergie's gum? Unless Roy Keane starts turning up to matches in cowboy boots it'll be a while until personal style makes such an impression from the dugout.

His departure is significant enough to prompt comment from figures as diverse as Gordon Brown and my mum – 'He made a huge impact in such a short time' and 'That dishy manager' respectively. Neither of them cared when Alan Pardew left West Ham.

We can glean from this momentous event several things: Abramovich will be satisfied with nothing less than immediate success in Europe, he wants attractive football and he wants to stick his oar in whenever he

David Humphries

fancies and put his mates in the team. One of the difficulties is that most of the great footballing dynasties have achieved success with practical, as opposed to flamboyant, football. Milan, Juventus and recent Real Madrid sides have prioritised winning over all else whereas teams like Barcelona or Arsenal always have moments of vulnerability and but two European Cup wins between them.

Personally, I'm sad about it. I've mentioned in this column before that Mourinho's presence at Chelsea prevented me from harbouring the hatred expected of a West Ham fan for our rivals across the capital because he provoked in me a kind of neutered lust. I enjoyed his aloof, snooty, manipulative interviews and eccentric outbursts; calling dear Wenger a voyeur and Frank Rijkaard a pervert. What about when he fled from police with his unquarantined lapdog? That's berserk, I can't imagine any other manager embarking on such a mad quest.

Sam Allardyce would not try to sneak his cat into a disco, David Moyes would never ride a cow to work and Alex Ferguson wouldn't squabble with cider tycoons over the ownership of a gee-gee. Actually he would because he too is a genius in the business of football management and in exchange for that bedazzling gift we'll tolerate his refusal to speak to the BBC, his hurling of boots at national treasures and his insistence on absolute authority at his club. But Abramovich wouldn't tolerate that, which is why when Chelsea visit Sir Alex Ferguson's Manchester United tomorrow it'll be under the stewardship of Avram Grant of whom I know little but suspect if Abramovich demanded his yacht play in goal and his wife on the wing would offer little resistance.

Like many a spurned lover before him Mourinho said he was going to take time off to unwind and wait for the phone to ring. I don't imagine he'll have long to wait till he gets optimistic tinklings from north and possibly east London and whatever he chooses to do I don't suppose it'll be long before he's back at the Bridge with a new paramour and then I suspect it'll be Abramovich who ends up heartbroken.

His Grace
Arsène, the
shaman of our
football

'I consider him a mystic, a shaman, an alchemist, speaking from somewhere far behind his inky eyes'

Six or seven games in we are able to ascertain the flavour of the season, we have savoured the first giddy sips and can now assess whether this shall be a vintage year. It'll be some time till we rinse away the spectacular taste of that swoonsome, dark rascal José Mourinho, probably we'll dispatch into the spittoon far sooner the bitter tang of Martin Jol, the poor sod, like a cuckolded father putting a brave face on for his bewildered kids, while Daniel Levy capers around Europe in a push-up bra with his knickers showing.

Fernando Torres is reckoned to be the new Ian Rush by Steven Gerrard and the arrival of the cartoonishly pretty Spaniard does seem significant. His input could ensure a realistic challenge from Merseyside for the first time in a decade-and-a-half and who but the blue faction of that city would begrudge them?

There is much to ponder in this richly evolving drama but my attention is drawn currently to Arsène Wenger, whose beautiful, more 'royal' than ever, Arsenal visit Upton Park tomorrow. Last season West Ham bested the Gunners twice, a feat that is unlikely to be repeated as Arsenal appear to have several teams playing with a grace, confidence and joy that is almost transcendental.

Given the concern that many expressed pre-season about post-Henry Arsenal this is a surprising and exciting development and one that can only really be attributed to Wenger, who to me seems to be vibrating above the frequency typically associated with our national game. I consider him a mystic, a shaman, an alchemist, speaking from somewhere far behind his inky eyes, issuing spiritual sermons on the game's decline and our obligation to nurture English talent.

Matt Johnstone

'English football's responsibility is to continue raising quality without losing its soul,' he says, talking of foreign money and bare terraces as potential symbols of an atheistic erosion of our holy essence. Ten years ago Wenger came over here, taking our jobs, recruited a clutch of Gallics and Latinos and picked up the Double with the insouciance of a gent collecting a baguette and an espresso. The debate continues to this day as to whether the influx of foreign talent has harmed our national team; I feel that if the game is elevated and standards raised that will ultimately be positive across all strata and few would dispute the contribution made by 'the professor' unless they are actual racists or Spurs fans.

Now that Wenger has expressed concern about the development of young English players it does seem more serious. But aside from his new ecclesiastical role he has no duty to anyone other than the fans and board of Arsenal and that doesn't run to positive discrimination in favour of Anglo-Saxons.

He spoke of fans as 'the keepers of the game' which is a further nod to the civic, if not sacred nature of the sport, which makes me query the new directive to referees to regard with renewed positivity 'hard to call' offside decisions, the reasoning being that 'a dodgy goal is preferable to a dodgy offside'. Is that an edict with which most fans would concur? Obviously that would be contingent on whether it was scored or conceded.

For me the relative scarcity of goals, perhaps the factor that has prevented football enchanting America, enhances their sanctity. Gary Lineker and his sexy, brown legs would never put the ball in the net in a pre-match kick-about so as not to tarnish the magic of that rarely achieved objective and in midweek I saw, in a match against Real Zaragoza, that paragon of the footballer as divine, Thierry Henry, on sighting a raised flag, curtail his magisterial canter towards goal with the despondency of a man abruptly woken from a beautiful dream.

It was as if, in that moment, meaning itself had been suspended, the ball with trickling inertia departed from its master, who himself was left to wonder, when would come his first goal in La Liga. Amidst the swirl of the scandals, the rumours, the ignoble chatter and limitless tainted money something chaste and sacred remains and it belongs to us, the fans and cannot be bought, sold or branded. Wenger is aware of this, which is why one can overlook the paucity of Englishmen in his side; he could field a team of ravens and be closer to the game's essence than most, and I hope, for West Ham's sake, that tomorrow he does.

9

Whatever next?
Joe Cole on stilts?

I'm in Tuscany. I've been sent here by my publishers to finish my autobiography. Usually, this column is the only writing obligation I have to fulfil and is rattishly indulged, today it must vie with literary siblings and is being produced during a hiatus of the solipsistic, caffeinated torrent that has consumed my every waking hour. Goethe wrote here, I am informed, and Auden too, so expectations are justifiably high and this voluptuous, rolling land ought to be sufficient muse for any man.

'Mourinho has the appearance of a gigolo assassin, Grant looks like Herman Munster's butler'

I went into town on Wednesday night to watch Chelsea vs Valencia, initially to gloat but as usual when abroad, was seduced by patriotism. My hopes that post-Mourinho Chelsea would fall apart looked likely to be fulfilled before a ball had been kicked, with John Terry in his see-through mask (there's a baffling concept, see-through masks. What's next? Cuddly daggers?) and Petr Cech in his stupid bonnet, they look like they're disintegrating as individuals let alone as a team. For future matches I want Joe Cole to be on stilts and Didier Drogba to wear fake boobies. Let Chelsea field a team of prosthetically enhanced oddities, it'll be good for morale.

After David Villa's opener I felt the first nationalistic twinge, the Italians that were watching were hardly vociferous, they indifferently sipped beer, but I took their silent boozing to be a slur upon Her Majesty and all her fleets and became enraged. 'How dare you!' I thought, after everything we've done for you. I began to crave a Chelsea revival, not in a profound way, just in a 'I drew them in a sweepstake at work' way. Then thanks to the skill and persistence of Drogba and Joe Cole, or Johkohl as he's known on Italian telly, Britannia triumphed.

Neil Fox

Were Chelsea more flamboyant under Avram Grant? It seems ridiculous that they could be, using the judge-a-book-by-its-cover method, Mourinho has the appearance of a Latino, gigolo assassin, Grant looks like Herman Munster's butler. There's a word that oughtn't to be bandied about so profligately, butler. Butler means a devoted, Woodhousian gentleman's gentleman. The lunatic who bears that title and has come as part of the package with this Tuscan villa would have seen Bertie Wooster starved and raped within an hour of his employment. I know that complaining about the quality of your butler is a lament unlikely to elicit much sympathy outside of Kensington but this fella, Sam, could no more butter me the perfect crumpet than take flight over the olive groves that surround me.

It was Sam who took us to the bar where we, me and my mate Nik (who's also my agent here to force me to write the booky wook), watched Wednesday's match and let me complain about the coffee and the light reflecting off the TV screen before telling me on the way home that the premises were run by the Mafia. I suppose I should be grateful he didn't wait till my funeral before mentioning it to my weeping mother.

Had I been aware that I was drinking in the Café Cosa Nostra I might not have been so cheeky with the waitresses, nor would I have sung the national anthem at the final whistle. The problem may be due to linguistic difficulties rather than incompetence – he did yesterday speak the sentence 'Marijuana Michelangelo my brother Italy.' I've been thinking about it ever since and am no closer to unravelling its mysteries.

What could it mean? It's almost entirely made of nouns, there's not a verb to be had. Could it mean that marijuana influenced the sculpture of Michelangelo and in turn inspired Sam and his brother to come to Italy? Whatever he said, it's better than my Italian, all I can say is 'grazi', I say it in different accents to deal with every situation. I just hope that I can intone 'grazi' in such a charming fashion that I can avoid being murdered in the plaza by a disgruntled Godfather.

Interview between Russell Brand and David Baddiel

DB: Y'know, I did have this complicated thing that I was going to talk to you about, but we're just going to talk about football, right?

RB: We can talk about the complicated thing as well as football if you want.

DB: Well, yeah, can you include in that complicated thing the creation of comedy as rock and roll in Britain, that has led directly to your career?

RB: I will – you may have noticed there is a rock and roll element in my persona. That is in no small part owing to David Baddiel, very much the John the Baptist to my Christ. Not only did you plant the seed for this comedy as the new rock and roll revolution, but this is a very specific favour you're doing me now, as it was you who suggested that we talk about the time we went to the England Croatia game where England famously lost and they didn't qualify for the European Championship.

DB: Yeah, we have to talk about that although obviously my abiding memory is depression exacerbated by the amount of very attractive women in the area that we were in who came up and offered you their phone numbers at a time when you

were supposed to be celibate as well, you'd made a public statement about your celibacy and yet in the … what's it called … the corporate section of Wembley, not really a hotbed of sexual activity, still I would say about eight women came up, all of them very attractive, and offered you their phone numbers, some of whom you may or may not have slept with, we probably can't go into that.

RB: It was the only way I could heal the scars of that horrific defeat.

DB: I probably wouldn't have minded on some level because obviously I was aware that going out into the open air with you that might happen but it was a particularly bad time for it to happen because I get genuinely depressed when England don't qualify or go out of major tournaments. So I feel I was particularly more indignant towards it than I might have been.

RB: And to heighten this sense of defeat and failure, here's a man enjoying the spoils of an idea of comedy that you've set up, right in front of your defeated face.

DB: I tell you though, because when England, I'm trying to keep it to football …

when England went out of Euro 96, when I was at perhaps the very height of my fame in England because everyone was singing my football song, one of the things I particularly remember, being with my then girlfriend and Frank Skinner being there with his then girlfriend, who was half German, and Frank Skinner basically in his relationship with her never really recovered from Germany defeating England on that day. So I suppose a small part of me might have been thinking, how can he be thinking about sex at a time like this when he should be full of rage, that you can't possibly be doing that. But you were doing that. I mean it's all rubbish because I would've been thinking about sex had the women been coming up to me but…

RB: Yeah.

DB: I'm just following the line of thought really.

RB: *(Laughter)* I was particularly proud to be at that England Croatia match with you and the defeat for me was all the more bitter on account of it meaning there wouldn't be a chorus of *Football's Coming Home*. Oh, that would be amazing if that happened, oh they'll see David and it will be really really exciting.

DB: Yeah, there was actually a small chance of that I think because it was a very important game, the England fans

don't really sing it anymore. I'm not entirely sure why. Well one reason is because England never play well enough. It's a strange football song in that respect in that it is only sung when England do well because *Football's Coming Home* implies that we are doing well, that the trophy is coming literally to our house, and if England aren't doing well it can't really be sung. And England haven't done well really for a long time and the only time I have heard it sung recently was when Germany played us and the German fans were singing it. Someone was with me and they said, 'Oh, they're singing your song,' and I feel hollow inside because I didn't actually put him right, I knew it was a German fan because Germany were doing well, and they said to me they're singing it, but I just left it because I wanted him to think that people still sung our song all the time.

RB: That's heartbreaking. I've always thought that that song has a flaw in that it's too triumphant thus restricting it to occasions of triumph, perhaps it could have done with a little more nuance…

DB: That's right, one of the strange things about the song is the reason it became a very big hit is that it was written in the spirit of melancholy because most other songs, England songs up to that point were, 'We're going to win it, we're coming home, we're off there to win it.'

RB: Yeah.

DB: When me and Frank talked about it we said, 'Let's write a song about what it's really like being an England fan which is, oh we're probably not going to win it but we sort of hope we are anyway.'

RB: That is four more years of hurt.

DB: Yeah, exactly, and it begins with you know 'everyone seems to know the score, we've heard it all before, England's going to throw it away, going to blow it away', all that stuff is about, oh well, no one thinks we're going to win but maybe we will anyway. But unfortunately the lines of triumph over adversity, 'football's coming home', which is the epiphany following that thought, they can only be sung when England are doing well.

RB: In a way David, yeah people wilfully took those lines out of context out of clear cockeyed optimism.

DB: I should've stood up at Wembley every time they sung it and said, 'No, you don't understand, it's a sweet, melancholy ballad about loss.'

RB: *(Laughter)*

DB: You've made it into a strident national anthem.

RB: It was a Jeff Buckley-style lament on the futility of football.

DB: Yeah. But anyway, what else do you want to know about football?

RB: Wait a sec … well, I've got a very lovely linking device because West Ham's song *Bubbles* is perhaps the only other song that captures the sort of sentimentality and pathos of being a football fan, as most songs do tend to be triumphant, and perhaps the team you follow, Chelsea, are a fine example of the kind of stripped-down refined success, lacking in magic but you know, under recent ownership, how do you define the romance of being a Chelsea fan for you at this time?

DB: Well … to start … the song *I'm Forever Blowing Bubbles*, is that a West Ham song, or is it just an old song that West Ham sing?

RB: I think it was, yeah I think it was co-opted.

DB: So what is it about when it's not about West Ham? I never know quite what it is … is it about someone who is blowing bubbles?

RB: *(Laughter)* It is quite difficult to find a literal connection, other than fortunes always hiding.

DB: Yeah, it is. But we sing it. We sing it as an anti-West Ham anthem which is about beating up, I believe, West Ham fans. How does it go? 'Tottenham always running, Arsenal running too', yeah, that's essentially the hooligan's anthem of course, so we've absorbed your song.

RB: I've heard the hooligan version David, and I'll go for a similar emotion that you've experienced when Germans sing *Football's Coming Home*. I think this is abuse of the lyrics from the intentions of the song.

DB: Yeah, I think it's a beautiful anthem, but to answer your question, I don't completely agree obviously with the Chelsea thing because having been a Chelsea fan since 1970, the only thing about being a Chelsea fan if you were a Chelsea fan then is that you were actually reared on a very stylish but rather pale form of play, so something very romantic which was Peter Osgood, Alan Hudson and Charlie Cooke, and all those kind of players being brilliant and stylish and clever but not actually winning very much, they won the FA Cup and the European Cup Winners' Cup but that was it. And then I went to Chelsea, I wasn't old enough to go when I started supporting them, when I was eleven and they were shit. They had Micky Droy in their team and they were utter shit and I went for twenty years watching them be complete shit and thus I actually get quite annoyed,

not as enraged as you do about your mum, and questions over her sexual endeavours but…

RB: Even you mentioning it now is making me a bit cross.

DB: Also I'm worried that the initial conversation won't be in the book and so people will think well why on earth has he said that, that's awful.

RB: No, we'll pick that out…

DB: But what I get annoyed about is the suggestion that this sort of wealth has somehow just landed on Chelsea fans unfairly whereas in fact when it first happened, I thought well this is actually Chelsea going back to its roots, because I think Abramovich, in his heart he wants Chelsea to be a bit like the Harlem Globetrotters, he wants them to be an incredibly skilful, exciting, flair-based club which he hasn't really chosen the managers to do.

RB: No.

DB: He's got that slightly wrong, but I think that's what he wants. And for Chelsea fans of my age there is a sense that we should be that club, you know, we should be this very flair, colourful club with lots of fancy dans like Peter Osgood playing for us, so I'm all for it. And I'm slightly fucked off that now that there are

Arabs at Manchester City who've got much more money than us.

RB: That must be irritating.

DB: That is irritating. I don't want to complain about it … well, perhaps slightly.

RB: Oh, go on.

DB: I've heard Chelsea fans…

RB: Go on, you were going to complain did you say? I'm listening…

DB: I've heard Chelsea fans complain, and they could be accused of hypocrisy here, that the Arabs at Manchester City are going to ruin football with all their money.

RB: *(Laughter)* Difficult to feel sympathy for the fans of Chelsea.

DB: Yeah it is, although it's a strange thing, you know, I've earned a fair amount of money in my time and you must be earning quite a lot now.

RB: Yeah.

DB: But these are people who can offer £138 million pounds for Ronaldo, just 'cos they sort of fancy it. How does that happen? How can people have that much money? It doesn't really reflect so much on football as the general state of the capitalist global economy.

RB: Yes that's what I feel. I feel that in general when people talk about the commercialisation of football, just say well this is cultural, that it's not something that is specific to football, it's just that demonstrably the world is becoming more corporate and more commercialised so of course sport is going to also, it's just a reflection of that.

DB: Yeah, that is true and football is a microcosm of the extreme nature of the free market because as football gets more and more successful, which it has done over the last fifteen years, more money is attracted to it. There aren't really any proper laws. The FA tried their best, but there aren't any proper laws like there might be in a country, so as a result there is a free-market activity leading to £138 million pounds which could probably save the whole of Africa being spent instead on Ronaldo and his stupid over-white teeth.

RB: I think you're quite right – instead of looking at football and condemning the current climate and the amount of money that players are earning, people should look at the implications of that globally, what that demonstrably means for global human capitalism.

DB: And they should also consider whether, if it is going to be a common, global economy Ronaldo should at least not be going to a club whose greatest player in the past was Francis Lee 'cos that in itself is an affront.

RB: *(Laughter)* Yeah, that is a peculiar poem of capitalism to go from Franny Lee to Ronaldo.

DB: It is, that's right, that is capitalism in itself, although somehow the movement from that fat bloke to that grinning pretty monkey is a remnant in some way of what Marx always predicted for our culture. I'm sure we're now just talking, aren't we?

RB: Yeah yeah we did, I felt we drifted away from making a football book to actual views and feelings.

DB: Ask me some other questions quickly about football.

RB: Ok.

DB: You're quite a big England fan, aren't you? That's the thing that people often talk about, club and country. And I feel from some of my, well Frank and the one or two other actually working-class friends that I've got, although you're actually working-class but you're not in this category, that there's something a bit poofty and middle-class about supporting England. I mean, Frank does support England but in his heart he will always say

he'd rather West Bromwich Albion got into the Premiership than England won the World Cup.

RB: Really?

DB: Now I don't know if I actually believe him, because I think he would go mental if England won the World Cup and West Brom have got into the Premiership and although he's pleased, he's not dancing naked in the street – a horrible image – but anyway he might do if England won the World Cup. So there's a sort of sense that comes off hardcore fans that supporting England is what Johnny-come-lately fans do – with their love of Italia 90 and Gazza crying and the whole change that happened in football, rather than the hardcore club supporters.

RB: That working-class affiliation, do you think it's by association – the hooligan fraternity as well, I know England have always famously had a hooligan fraternity? That sort of class ownership of the sport is kind of interesting, I mean I would like to pick up on that 'cos Frank is personally affiliated with the success of England. If England won the World Cup, I'd imagine it would be like twenty or thirty years in the future before it's possible at all, you two would be pushed out on wheelchairs with Ian Broudie, it would be a personal triumph for you as well like a cultural and social one.

DB: One of those people who are wheeled out on Remembrance Day.

RB: Yeah.

DB: And we'd have to sing the song in our creepy old voices.

RB: Oh, with tears in your eyes. And I'd like to think that by then you'd have somehow lost an arm and you'd have your sleeve pinned to your jacket.

DB: *(Laughter)* Somehow I'd been involved in the Great War.

RB: *(Laughter)*

DB: Yeah, and we'd be singing it like it was the *Last Post*.

RB: *(Laughter)* Because I feel that the paradigm of supporting West Ham is almost perfectly replicated by supporting England. You think, 'Oh yeah, it's gonna be triumph, it's going to be absorbed in a cup run or a signing,' but ultimately it will inevitably lead to defeat and disappointment. Like Irvine Welsh feeling that in their hearts everyone secretly would prefer to support Hibs, he really believes that, and that there's something about Hibs that everyone secretly, no matter what they say, thinks Hibs is much cooler.

DB: There's something magical about Hibs? I think Irvine Welsh is wrong about that. I certainly never wanted to support Hibs or indeed watch Scottish football in any way, even as a kid, when they used to have the Scottish results I used to think why, why do we have to have this? In England, no one is interested in what Queen of the South did.

RB: No. I remember as a child thinking what a bizarre litany of words Kilmarnock, Partick Thistle…

DB: One of our greatest jokes in *The Mary Whitehouse Experience*, you probably don't remember, involved that. Because we had a sketch where the bloke who used to read out the football results was at home and of course he speaks in a reading-out-the-results way all the time…

RB: Oh yeah?

DB: I really like this joke which is, he is asked 'What do you think of John Inman?' And he says, 'He's not just Queen of the North, he's Queen of the South too.'

RB: *(Laughter)*

DB: And I remember thinking, 'I'm very pleased with that.'

RB: *(Laughter)*

DB: But er … what was I saying? Yes…

RB: I can't remember anything after that spectacular joke. It was a condemnation of Scottish football there which people will have to tiptoe around and take bits out of.

DB: Yeah.

RB: And then…

DB: It's all right, you can condemn Scottish football because the Scots hate us, they hate me and Frank because of that strange thing. It's a bit like what you're talking about, the tribalism which football inspires. Which is why I think there is the club vs country thing, you know, more self-consciously hardcore fans prefer clubs because it allows them to be more tribal. There's more a kind of hate, there's more sense of local ownership and all that stuff. That's why Man United fans are sneered at for not being from Manchester you know, it harks back to an older idea of community where people actually supported their local stuff and their local area, which don't really exist anymore but people wish it would. People wish life was like it is in *The Royle Family*, not the real Royal Family, the one that Caroline Aherne wrote. Anyway, what am I talking about…?

RB: Tribalism and Scottish pride over the…

DB: The thing about Scotland that is really a remnant of that, is that Scottish fans hate England and England fans. Since we wrote *Three Lions*, whenever I have gone to Scotland some cunt will shout 'Cunt' at me, or Frank if I'm with him, for writing that. Sometimes they're friendly, sometimes it's a bit more aggressive in the manner of Scottish people. And it's interesting that there is no hatred back really. When we were children I was taught to support Scotland in 1974 and 1978 because England weren't in the World Cup. And it never occurred to me to think, well I can't because I hate Scotland.

RB: *(Laughter)*

DB: But of course, the Scots would never have supported England in all the times that Scotland haven't got to the World Cup and England have, and therefore it's a very interesting example of football tribalism because I always want to say to those Scottish fans, 'Well, you make yourself look stupid by hating a country and a football team that doesn't hate you back, you know.'

RB: Yes, one-sided hate is almost as tragic as unrequited love because it's an equally onanistic relationship. But I think, David, that the point you've made there is again the point where football becomes a reflection of culture at large. It's just that football provided an outlet for their anti-English sentiments and the geographical, historical and military reasons for that and just provided a template, whereas England don't have any of those grievances because of the oppression that we've applied to them. Stuart Lee did a very good joke when Jimmy Hill tried to defend Ron Atkinson's racist remarks by saying that the things Ron Atkinson said about, um, Marcel Desailly, 'Oh, it's the same as when I get called Chinny.' And Stuart Lee continued that, well, it's not really, because there's not a long history of big-chinned people being oppressed and abused by the white man, and he continued that analogy for as long as he could.

DB: ...and the comedy being about breaking a butterfly upon a wheel as it so often is with Stuart Lee, but yes he is correct about that.

RB: And isn't that similar to what you're saying about Scotland in that hatred is actually a reflection of something cultural and football has really become the canvas on which that is played out?

DB: Football is very interesting in the way that it can reflect culture in that way. That the reason Scottish fans hate England, it's a way of creating their own identity through that hate. If you're a small country with a bigger country nearby that you feel oppressed by, one way of creating your identity is to hate that country. In the list of what makes a Scottish person Scottish, hating England

is probably up there after kilts and haggis. And so it must be because England doesn't quite have that. That hating another country makes us what we are thing. Although it does have it a bit because I think a lot of English people now hate America, don't they?

RB: Right.

DB: Not all of them but you'll see a lot of anti-Americanism, especially from the British Left. I think that is partly the same thing. It's about, right ok, we don't have an empire anymore, how can we create a British identity for ourselves, let's hate all together and communally this country which is now much bigger and more important than us. I think we're moving slightly away from football but I think football shows it in a different way. It's important to Arsenal fans that they hate Tottenham, that's part of what makes an Arsenal fan isn't it? It's not just where you come from or liking Arsène Wenger or remembering Herbert Chapman.

RB: Yeah, if you were to say, I am an Arsenal fan but also I quite like Tottenham, it would undermine you as an Arsenal fan.

DB: I don't know what it is with West Ham, but Chelsea don't really have an object point of hatred. There is a strong anti-Semitic section of Chelsea, who will shout 'Yiddo' at Tottenham fans and will start shouting 'We hate Tottenham and we hate Tottenham', but I always feel that they have a slight inferiority complex about it, because they don't hate Tottenham as much as Arsenal do.

RB: It's strange, isn't it, because West Ham fans 'Hate Tottenham, we hate Tottenham, we are Tottenham haters'. But when it comes to hating Tottenham, you can't beat Arsenal.

DB: Arsenal have the advantage of being geographically closer to Tottenham than either West Ham or Chelsea so they could even manage to do it. The people that we have to hate locally are QPR and Fulham who are not up to scratch for hating because they're too small.

RB: It'd be no fun hating QPR or Fulham. Of course West Ham fans 'Hate Millwall, hate Millwall'. I know to the ICS fraternity that would be like hugely relevant and I think there's been deaths involved it's been taken so seriously. But for a bog-standard football fan that sort of hatred becomes kind of spurious and irrelevant, because other than the occasional cup tie, there is no chance to play out that confrontation. I'm not gonna ever go to New Cross to express my hatred to Millwall.

DB: It's a very interesting thing though, particularly for me and you as football fans because I never could do that. I was

never very bothered with hating anyone, actually I used to vaguely hate Arsenal when George Graham was their manager 'cos they played really dull football and beat us and that was annoying, but when they started playing really brilliant football I thought, 'Well I don't hate them anymore because there isn't anything to hate,' any more than any other team that played Chelsea. And actually I sort of appreciated the fact that Vieira and Henry are brilliant players and I quite respect them, and I can't bring myself to hate them just to confirm my identity as a Chelsea fan. And similarly you, the part of you that is a bit hippy and a bit karmic and who hates Mourinho.

RB: And is attracted to him.

DB: Yeah.

RB: This is not a sanctioned emotion of a West Ham fan.

DB: …about José Mourinho, I believe I texted you to say something about you and your issues with stepfathers.

RB: Yeah.

DB: With Avram Grant I think that was a general mass psychosis. Although clearly Avram Grant wasn't as good a manager as José Mourinho – the absolute hatred of him both from Chelsea fans and generally, he was thought of as useless by everybody despite getting us to the European Cup Final. I think the mass psychosis was about how we had this really cool, really dynamic high-status but somehow charming and lovable perfect kind of modern father figure, but paternal but actually quite modern and cool and handsome and all the rest of it, and then this sort of silly old frog-like bloke took over.

RB: *(Laughter)*

DB: And it was a terrible revulsion – who is this man supposedly looking after us now and even you felt it from West Ham, even though I think you had deeper psychological issues.

RB: Yeah.

DB: You have father issues which we won't go into.

RB: Yeah, let's psychoanalyse that particular problem. A whole nation did say, 'You're not my real dad.'

DB: Yeah, they said 'You're not my real dad,' exactly. *(Laughter)*

RB: You can't tell us what to do, you can't take us to the European Champions League Final.

DB: Exactly, especially with that face. I'm going to have to go, Russell.

RB: All right then.

DB: Because I have to go and see a play, so I would love to talk to you more but I can't really.

RB: All right.

DB: So um…

RB: That's fantastic, thank you David. Thanks for ending it, leaving me with that chilling image of my problems around patriarchy.

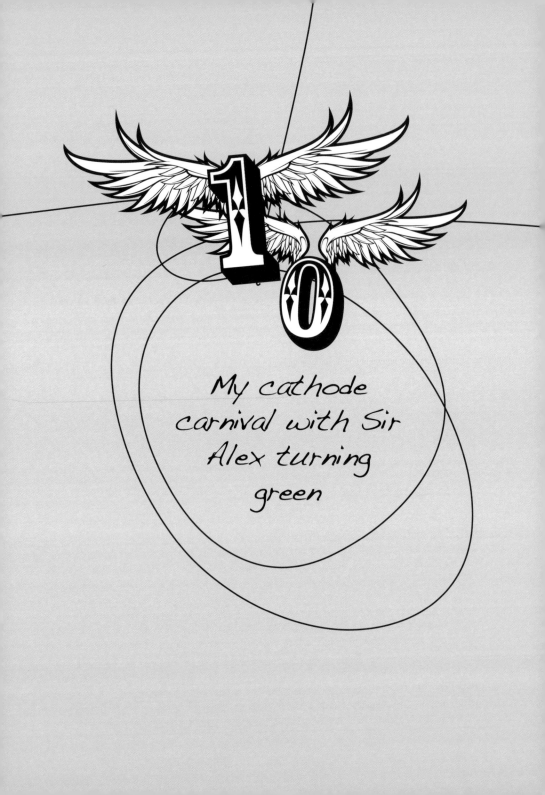

10

My cathode
carnival with Sir
Alex turning
green

I'm still in Tuscany writing my autobiography. Who would've thought that writing a book that covers the expanse of your entire life would be so time consuming? It's nearly finished now and it's jolly good. A cursory glance, not that I'm suggesting that's the manner in which it ought be read, reveals that football has been little more than a pain-in-the-arse recruitment officer for disappointment and despair ever since it sauntered into my life in the early 80s.

I was old enough to understand the concept of football for the World Cup in Spain '82 but it wasn't till Mexico '86 that I became fully able to contend with the hopelessness and vindictive failure that our nation is expected to tolerate during international competition. England seem to do better when I either harshly criticise them or stay out of the country and ignore them.

'Michael Owen seems to be responding to the English press like the child of an unreliable, alcoholic parent'

The only portals to information accessible to me here are day-old newspapers – I now pretend that the days are synchronised and ignore calendars to avoid feeling out of touch. The internet simply will not work here, our lying 'butler' Sam, who I mentioned last week in his capacity as a goon likely to get me bumped off by Tuscan mafiosi, claims that Italy does not have the internet while maintaining eye contact and chuckling.

The TV, when operable, is about as reliable as the butler and last week we watched the world-famous greens of Manchester United finally hit their stride against Wigan. We've got an expressionistic telly that gives you its own bonkers interpretation of colour and in its bonkers cathode carnival red equals green. All the colours are subverted and shuffled, a lot of them randomly – the Wigan players turned out in a strip that would please only

Benetton – but it is quite consistent in its red to green ideal. On our TV the United shirts and Sir Alex Ferguson's face are both the same hue of shimmering jade, like the scales of a marlin. I'm starved of reliable media, the papers are late, the internet doesn't exist and the television is increasingly Dadaist.

This means that I am an ideal case study for Chomsky's ideas on the manufacture of consent. My emotions are tossed around on a tabloid sea of vituperation and rumour. One paper announces that Frank Lampard will soon be leaving Chelsea, another that Kaká will be arriving. Is that an example of how a Premiership club's PR operations are run? If one paper

has a story of a departing hero another must be fed one of an imminent superstar arrival?

Poor bloody Michael Owen; he seems to be responding to the English press like the child of an unreliable, alcoholic parent; nothing he does is good enough and it's impossible for him to pre-empt how his actions will be received. I'm glad he's back from injury and so keen to play, and that recent international results have meant that he's been reinstated as our football Jesus.

The last two positive results ought to have been taken as evidence that England perform well when adhering to a team ideal rather than facilitating individuals. Perhaps it's because we still live in a monarchic culture that we crave a talismanic figure to praise and condemn and struggle to appreciate the importance of a balanced team. I hope this pervasive tendency doesn't diminish the likelihood of Gareth Barry's inclusion; judging from what I've read, he is the very kind of player that could help England evolve.

Of course, all of my opinions are gleaned from day-old news, for all I know I could've overslept or been drugged and missed another few days or even weeks, and England might already have beaten Estonia and Russia. Perhaps Sam the Butler savant has been printing all these papers himself and has created for me an insular wonderland. I did read that Sven-Goran Eriksson is having sex with a dustbin man – that seems unlikely – and that Britain is in the thrall of an alleged terrorist called 'Osama Bin London'. Absurd. These things can't be true.

Well, whatever the hell it is that's going on over there, good luck England and Michael and Gareth. And if Sven is tucking into a bit of rough while a punning fundamentalist causes havoc I might stay here another couple of weeks and watch the games on TV. Come on you greens.

11

Who's to blame
for my impotent
rage?

Desolate. The evisceration makes analysis appear futile. Vivid recollection torments the fastidious mind, unwilling to relinquish detail. The un-penalty – I frantically write optimistic headlines in my mind, Robinson Redeems Himself With Heroic Save – then the disappointment. The familiar cosy acceptance of yet another defeat.

Whilst we were one up for that unrealistic hour I felt the defeat gestating in my belly with every tick-tock of the inevitable clock, like when West Ham led Liverpool 2–0 in Cardiff last year; the score seemed absurd. I was relieved when Liverpool got one back because the single goal advantage was more manageable.

This sense of foreboding and tragic destiny is now our only comfort as we confront the likely absence of our national side from next year's championship. I find it hard to condemn Steve McClaren. My facile rage rains impotently on his cadaver as furious blows rendered in a dream. It's not his fault, I may as well rail against my cat for his inability to cook authentic Thai food.

'When have we ever had a handsome England boss? Glenn Hoddle? Kevin Keegan?'

McClaren was never the man for the England job, yet I too joined the illusion after the three consecutive 3–0 victories. I conjured tableaux of trophies held above his head, glowing with triumph in addition to the glow it perpetually maintains. Even in this, a time of terrible defeat, the McClaren bonce glows on, a beacon of gleaming mediocrity.

It's too soon for me to become giggly and receptive to the possibility of a romance with José Mourinho or Martin O'Neill; Mourinho won't take it, he's too dashed handsome – when have we ever had a handsome England boss? Glenn Hoddle? Kevin Keegan?

I don't know if I can summon up the gusto to hope for Israel to produce a result, I've reached a familiar point where, through self-pity, I can see little point in progression: 'We don't deserve to qualify.'

I still cringe at the memory, decades old, of an infant chastisement – whilst out with a school friend and his mum I carried on in my typical picaresque fashion, flicking rubber bands and pocketing gobstoppers.

Adrian Johnson

I was told off by my mate's mum. Naturally I was shocked and unnerved, as is always the case when a foreign authority exercises control, and I collapsed into tears. Later, when the dust had settled, consolation chocolate bars were offered. 'I don't deserve one,' I sobbed, not entirely sincerely but with litres of sentimentality, sentimentality; the unearned emotion. Perhaps England need another wilderness period.

Like in 1994 when we didn't travel to the States for the World Cup. I hate it though, it's rubbish when England don't qualify; watching the games through a transparent pain of regret and bitterness. I can't focus, every kick and whistle a taunt, an indiscreet reminder of our absence. Who can we blame? The pitch?

Those bloody plastic pitches. When QPR and Luton used to have them it was a constant source of resentment, spoken of through clenched teeth. 'That bloody AstroTurf,' we all agreed, 'it's bad for the game.' I don't remember, in those days of the old First Division, the sides in question watering their plastic pitches though; that's a bit baffling.

Surely one of the advantages, and may I stress unfair advantages, of having a plastic pitch is that you don't have to water it or talk to it or fertilise it; the whole caper reeks of foul play. We could blame the referee for the penalty, which was palpably outside of the box, but then Wayne Rooney's goal was offside anyway so we can't even be righteously aggrieved by that unfair decision.

The FA, can we blame them? I suppose so but what's the point, lovely old doddering sods they are, just trying to get through life. They'll be penalised as much as anyone by the financial implications of not qualifying. Sponsorship and advertising money all nonsense now.

We shall spend next summer trapped in our impoverished nation, peeping through a crack in the curtain as the rest of Europe indulges in an orgy of sport with our national game; swarthy Italians, sophisticated Frenchmen or possibly even joyful Scots caressing and fondling our balls because we don't know how to look after them. Never have I felt more irritated by my inherited indifference to rugby.

First rule for life
in the lounge:
no swearing

Tony Cottee requested that I be his guest in the lounge for West Ham's last home game against Sunderland. In this context 'being a guest in the lounge' is not like it would be in *Lady Windermere's Fan* where one would sit demurely exchanging epigrams with toffs. No, what it entails is appearing on a low-budget chat show, where you stand – that's right, stand, I said it was low-budget – and are interviewed by Tony before an audience of West Ham fans tucking into their nosh.

One suspects that the sedentary diners have paid handsomely for this unique afternoon of entertainment and I was determined not to let them, or Tony, down. Cottee is a hero of mine, occupying a place in my affections so formative that it is almost impossible to view him objectively. He exists in a realm shared by childhood pets, Worzel Gummidge and Morrissey; a realm that precedes rational judgment, for the retina of my consciousness was scorched by his image before the facility to analyse had evolved.

'I'm still a bit angry with the tennis player lady post-pubescently. Why didn't she put knickers on?'

Like when I first saw that poster of the tennis player lady scratching her bottom it made me feel angry as at that early stage I didn't know how to be aroused. Actually, I'm still a bit angry with her post-pubescently – why didn't she put some knickers on if she knew she was going to be playing tennis? It's flouting the sport's conventions.

When I think of all the bother Andre Agassi endured at Wimbledon just for wearing those colourful cycling shorts it makes my blood boil. At least he didn't turn up on Centre Court nude from the waist down dragging himself along the baseline like dogs do to scratch their arses. It's one rule for the rich and one for the poor.

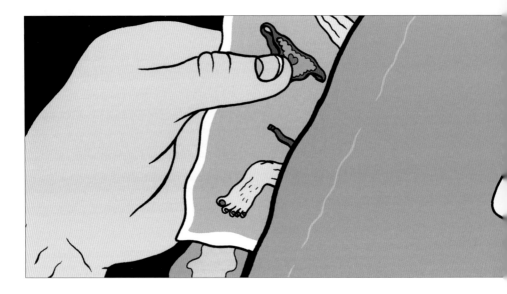

So with all that borne in mind you can imagine it was important I didn't disappoint TC. He runs the executive lounges at Upton Park with the same febrile tenacity that he ran West Ham's attack in the 80s, and he stoutly issued me with instructions: there are two lounges, we do them consecutively, Tony does the quiz and player of the month (my current heartthrob Mark Noble) then brings me out for a chat.

He asks me five questions – 'No pressure, it's just a laugh' – then we repeat the process in the second lounge. Oh, and 'No swearing'. Simple. Here are just some of the blunders I managed to jam into my five-minute interview in lounge one:

a) I said that I thought Dean Ashton would be influential even though Dean is currently out with a knee injury. Damn. I've been away for weeks in Tuscany with no internet or papers writing my autobiography. I was oblivious. I'm so sorry;

b) I implied that in the legendary partnership between Tony and my beloved Frank McAvennie, Tony was a goal scrounger while Frank did all the running, deftly comparing it to the onstage relationship between myself and the show's esteemed host;

Matt Johnstone

c) To illustrate the nature of man's curiosity I evoked an analogy in which I queried whether the audience would open an envelope which contained a photograph of Her Majesty The Queen's vagina.

And, finally, d) I said 'fuck'. Before we embarked on the second lounge Tony's main note was 'watch the swearing', he was quite firm about it, then during interview two, which was better, as I went to relay my royal analogy Tony expertly steered me into some chat about Billy Bonds.

And then to watch the match. I sat with Tony, his mate John and his lovely dad Clive to witness West Ham's flattering 3–1 victory against the 'Black Cats' (I struggle with that nickname as it was only issued as the result of a poll in a local paper in Sunderland and I query whether or not actual Sunderland fans use it conversationally. Or if they're too self-conscious thinking maybe they should've gone down a less obvious route of talismans for ill fortune in a blatant affront to their rivals Newcastle United's nickname 'the Magpies') more shy about chanting than usual and profoundly touched that a man whom I used to study with awe as a child as he hustled defences and keepers and scored now sat beside me watching the team we both love.

13

East will always
be east for lovers
of freedom

EAST EAST East London. EAST EAST East London. It's a simple enough chant, a peculiarly forceful and evocative ditty only relevant in the minute context of Upton Park for West Ham's home games and for tiny allocated corners elsewhere when away. I mention it only in an attempt to popularise the lyric as the two 'EASTS' that precede 'East London' were immolated by a copy reader at the publisher of my forthcoming autobiography *My Booky Wook* – serialised in this paper a week Monday.

I was describing my early visits to the Boleyn ground with my Dad, and put '. . . on weekend trips to EAST EAST East London . . .' as a coded message to the claret and blue army. This was taken by the copy reader as evidence that she was dealing with the absent-minded doodlings of a mental patient and she swiftly exorcised the sentence of its charm so it reads simply '. . . trips to East London . . .'

'The only way to run a club is as a dictatorship. Witness the top flight's Stalin and Mao, Ferguson and Wenger'

Now of course my autobiography, like the homework of a recalcitrant berk, was handed in about 20 seconds before the book was due to go to print meaning there was no time for this error to be corrected. I suppose this lady, having read a substantial portion of the booky wook by this stage, had due cause to suspect she was not editing the work of an infallible literary force and having weathered a torrent of evidence of insanity took this to be a kind of needless outburst of Touret-tic orienteering lingo rather than a sweet nod to a menacing chorus. These things happen. A trivial, accidental injustice that has speared its way into the malignant core of my creativity and lanced the tumour of furious perfectionism that festers therein. These things happen. I suppose it doesn't really matter – it wasn't the defining sentence of the book – but it's

Neil Fox

difficult to quarrel with one's own feelings, and I feel browned off.

That big, lovely, bald Honey Monster of a man Martin Jol apparently experienced similar duress when at the Lane, he endured Damien Comolli giving him an unwelcome reach-round while he was trying to bring his squad to climax. Jol revealed that he planned to bring Manchester City hits Elano and Martin Petrov (it's easy to say that now, I've always loved Sven myself, never once suggesting that he joined England players in the post-match bath wearing soggy knickers) to Spurs but Comolli brought in players that would have long-term commercial re-sale value like Darren Bent (we'll all be rich, I tells ya) and Adel Taarabt.

It can't be much fun trying to manage a Premier League team of teenage millionaires while the club chairman and director of football (which is a job title to undermine a manager's control if ever I heard one – 'Don't mind me, I'll just be here directing the football') stand just behind you pulling 'spaz' faces and doing 'wanker' signs. Why not just turn up at first-team training sessions and stick Post-its on Martin's back reading 'I want my Mummy' or put cards in phone boxes with his mobile number and 'I will bend over for cash' written on them.

The only way to run a Premier League club is as a dictatorship. Witness the top flight's own Stalin and Mao, Ferguson and Wenger, answerable to no one, sat beyond reproach atop the power pyramid of their respective clubs, Titans answerable only to God and their own consciences. May I just point out that I'm not implying that either man is genocidal, it's simply not called for in their line of work, but I can't imagine Sir Alex would take kindly to anybody abbreviating his autobiography – although his life isn't littered with evidence of instability, unless he really did throw that shoe at David Beckham and even that's not as bad as the ice pick that Trotsky had to contend with just for trying his hardest.

So, try and use EAST EAST East London as often as you can till it's as popular an idiom as Whassup! Or Milf. Make sure you find an appropriate situation, though, or people will think you're nuts.

14

My view from
afar of Fergie's
flirtatious
feuding

I'm in Morocco and no matter how completely my senses are flooded with the mystery of the souks and the nobility of the Atlas mountains this will always be to me the nation that in Mexico '86 fielded a player called Mustafa Merry (I remember the Panini sticker book representation rather than the individual). I liked that name as a child as it seemed like a joke, and also pre-empted by a decade my mate Matt's nickname for me as an Arabic tunic-wearing junkie, Mustafa Skagfix.

The other prejudice I've been carting about was learned from the Joe Orton biopic *Prick Up Your Ears* where Joe and his murderous lover Kenneth Halliwell briefly holidayed here and copped off with loads of rent-boys. I don't know why that stayed with me, it just seemed so jolly, bathing costumes, giggling and Alfred Molina and Gary Oldman enjoying tense frissons. The memory of the pair of them, and Mustafa Merry, skipped through my mind while I was on the phone to the travel agent.

'It's like flirting a bit, or any form of seduction: one must destabilise the target to make them suggestible to new ideas'

I've not encountered Mustafa or a single rent-boy the whole time I've been here and am thinking of demanding a discount. I've kept my eye on things in Albion though and here's my round-up of football news, not to mention my 'wacky, sideways' view of it all: Chris Hutchings's sacking; oh. I liked him, he was a friendly peep-eyed, thin-lipped, gel-haired uncle and I don't think Dave Whelan has given him long enough. Also talk of Paul Jewell returning to Wigan seems barmy because Hutchings was formerly his first-team coach.

What if Jewell does return and offers Hutchings his old job back? It'll be uncomfortable, Hutchings won't be able to tell the players anything – he'll be like a castrated step-dad. 'Run round them cones lads,' he might shout; 'Eff off, you're not my real coach,' Heskey'll respond. It'll be awful. It doesn't do to go backwards, unless you're an old lady descending stairs, then it's de rigueur.

West Ham have always been keen on the ol' 'sell players then bring 'em back' technique and it's always a bit disappointing. Julian Dicks, Tony Cottee and Frank McAvennie all came back for less successful second spells and whilst it's romantic I don't know that it's good business. Though who wouldn't welcome dear Harry Redknapp back to the Boleyn in an instant? Why, only the loopy and the indifferent.

There was talk of Nicolas Anelka returning to Arsenal but I imagine Arsène Wenger is not one given to nostalgia, and it seems improbable that any of Fergie's former charges would be welcome back at Old Trafford – they usually seem to be kicked out from 'neath the protection of his coarse petticoats like incestuous toddlers.

David Humphries

I admire Sir Alex Ferguson's need for conflict as much as his appetite for success, and his remarks this week about Sepp Blatter's proposed cap on foreign players were tremendous fun; implying that Arsenal and

Liverpool would suffer most under such a ruling then nonchalantly awaiting the protestations from the Emirates.

Wenger was of course unable to resist retaliating and I thought his riposte was a good one: 'His own foreign players must feel undervalued by that.' I enjoyed this particularly as I was following this minor dispute as if it were a soap opera and after Ferguson's initial dig I knew Wenger would respond but was unable to anticipate the quality of his parry. It's like flirting a bit, or any form of seduction: one must destabilise the target to make them suggestible to new ideas, like bumming.

Not that I'm suggesting that this was Ferguson's ulterior motive although the chemistry between them is exciting. The cursory, eye-contact-free handshake that followed last Saturday's clash, whilst brief, must have felt enormous to either man. Like having a fingernail traced up the nape of your neck or sweet breath blown into your ear, how could it not engender an electric shudder? I wonder if they think about each other much when they're alone, initially angry – 'the security was a bloody joke' – but lapsing into the whimsical – 'he has such inviting lips, ever wet and puckered, each rebuke a prelude to a vicious kiss' – almost certainly.

Actually Yossi Benayoun would be carried shoulder high along the Barking Road should he ever return. His hat-trick against Besiktas, like every ball Joe Cole has ever kicked whilst clad in blue, induced a gut-pang, and now as a nation we must hope that he uses his much missed and lamented skills to give England a chance of qualifying for the European Championship perhaps, if the mischievous deities of nostalgia have their way, under the stewardship of Terry Venables.

15

I need a new
way to feed my
England habit

When organising warm-up gigs for the forthcoming, final leg of my current tour my tour manager, Ian (City), and manager, Nik (United), asked if I wanted to keep Wednesday night free for the England match. Whether the game against Croatia is of any relevance will be determined tonight in Tel Aviv when Israel play Russia – if Russia don't win then England can still qualify for the European Championship with a victory against the group leaders at Wembley.

In effect, my response to this inquiry will define me either as a patriotic optimist or an indifferent pessimist. Or, as is often the case in these times, there is a third way: I could remain essentially optimistic but affiliate myself only with the claret and blue corner of England where Bow Bells chime and bubbles blow, like a Cornish separatist imagining new borders around a principality of the heart.

'Only 38 Englishmen played in the Premiership. I don't want to get all Oswald Mosley but is that enough?'

We all know of the pledge, of course, where we swear to never again be seduced by a national side that only ever lets us down, an oath that is easier to remain faithful to if you're a fan of Manchester United or Arsenal and have a happy and successful domestic football life than if you follow Huddersfield, no disrespect, or even West Ham. But perhaps that constituency is now being diminished. Fans of the MK Dons could find more joy and triumph following their local team than by going to all the bother of daubing a St George's Cross with Milton Keynes and traipsing off to Vienna.

I can't seem to give up my England habit: although I've never seen them play I have been inveigled by the trappings. Esso World Cup coins, for example, which bore the faces of the Italia 90 squad were as prized as richly as golden doubloons by my teenage self and while people fret and query the benefits of adopting the euro I campaign tirelessly in my mind to have them made our sole legal tender – a Peter Beardsley for a loaf of bread, a Chris Waddle for a day pass at Thorpe Park and a weeping Gazza for unlimited lap dances at Spearmint Rhino (they were very rare).

Last week only 38 Englishmen played in the Premiership. Now I don't want to get all Oswald Mosley but is that enough? We're approaching the point where if you are a top-flight English footballer you can assume you'll be in the squad, just turn up at the airport in your PE kit and demand a chance. So perhaps Michel Platini and the brave Steven Gerrard are right, that there ought to be a cap on foreign players or players should run out for the nation in which they earn their money.

That might be quite good actually, not just because then 'England' would be bloody brilliant but also David Beckham would have to play for the United States, probably as skipper, affording me the delightful opportunity to write an article entitled 'Captain America to the rescue' which would be a breeze. It might even help to loosen the stranglehold that nationalism still has upon us, and our atavistic tribal instincts, to the point where we abandon the concept of the individual and gather in stadiums just to cheer the idea of collective consciousness – it would be much harder to tell who'd won or when the game had finished and some people would still struggle with the offside rule but it might herald an age of global peace.

When I was a lad and Liverpool won everything, folk would harp on about Sammy Lee being the only English player because that side was made up largely of home nations players. Others would say he was like a little barrel that had come to life in a Disney film set in a brewery but they contribute nought to this argument and can just eff off.

I suppose what I'm saying is that England will always underachieve, and it doesn't seem to be something we can correlate to club football in a direct way. If we don't qualify there is talk of having a home nations tournament, presuming that Scotland are also available, and some of my mates are more into that idea. 'Four meaningful matches,' said John

Paddy Molloy

(Liverpool) and I'd be interested to watch such a tourney, but it might feel a bit like the third-place matches in the World Cup where two teams of disillusioned failures vie for mediocrity.

We'd be pretending to care about our mini-matches but actually in our heart of hearts we'd know we were watching a consolation cup, for little girls in their mum's high-heels tottering around, fancying themselves all adult but not contributing to the gas bill.

I'm doing my warm-up gigs on Monday and Tuesday night and keeping Wednesday free because I make decisions with my heart (especially now my goolies are out of action) so Wednesday I'll be watching England and I hope it'll be consequential. I know it'll be a lot more relaxed than the front room in Yarm where Steve McClaren will watch tonight's other group matches with his sons and a loudly ticking clock.

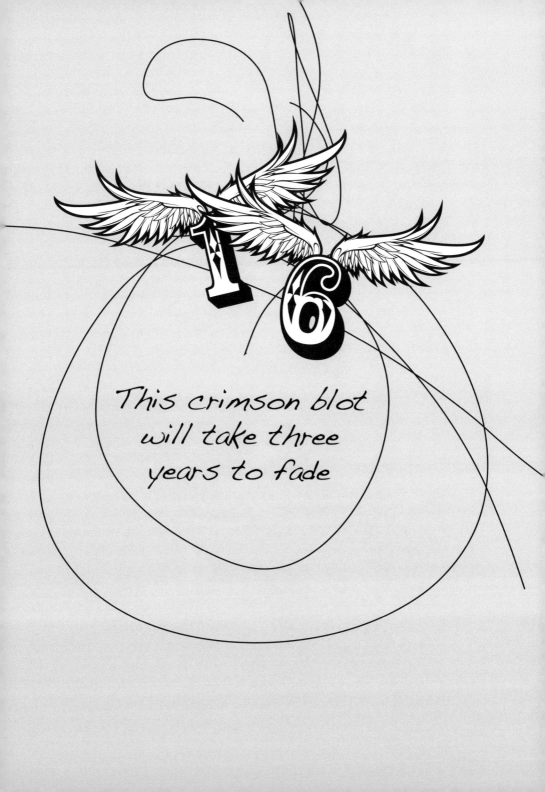

This crimson blot
will take three
years to fade

I first became anxious when I realised that beneath the twirling, hypnotic umbrella seeking shelter from the lightly drizzling rain permitted by the broken roof at Wembley stood the manager of our national team, Steve McClaren. I was at the match in incredible seats with my mate Nik and David Baddiel and his brother Ivor.

We were right behind the dugout in posh leather-look seats having enjoyed the delightful hospitality of one of the lounges which was a bit embarrassing for us all in the sense that it's quite far removed from the authentic trudge and bilge that's synonymous with the football of our youth. Actually though I do like a bit of luxurious nosh and privilege in this the final flush of capitalism before the revolution levels us all, a revolution that seems all the more attractive now the beautiful distraction of Euro 2008 has been smashed to bits.

'I bumped into a Croat in the lavvy and was unready for good-natured prittle-prattle so I neglected to ablute'

It seems daft to harp on about the subsidiary consequences of England's failure to qualify because the immediate effects are so upsetting; after a knife wound to the heart one is unlikely to lament the blood stains on your T-shirt and this crimson blot will take at least three years to rinse away. I wonder if Brian Barwick'll feel embarrassed in South Africa at the World Cup qualifiers draw? If he'll avoid the pitying glare and condemnation from his counterparts?

I bumped into a Croat in the lavvy straight after the match and was still unready for good-natured prittle-prattle so I neglected to ablute to avoid handshakes. I bore them ill-will even before the final whistle because of what I perceived to be a needlessly fascistic form of chanting throughout the match. Perhaps this says more about my prejudices than the philosophy of those fans but it did seem terribly well organised – two huge, adjacent sections of the stadium spent the entirety of the match indulging in a terrifyingly simplistic call-and-response mantra that unnerved me as much as the sharp, acerbic presence of Slaven Bilić on the touchline first in a woolly hat and an awful off-white coat that the whole Croatian operation had been forced to wear, then when he re-emerged for the second half, assured of victory, in a shoddy suit.

Why I've reserved my vituperation for this obviously talented manager and former West Ham centre-half is a mystery when a more fitting candidate for wrath stood like Gene Kelly or more latterly Rihanna meekly concealed beneath his brolly awaiting a holiday in the Bahamas that it turns out he'd already booked. I was distracted in that fabulous stadium. David was agitated by the fact that the roof hadn't been closed and queried whether it was a misjudged tactical flooding under the assumption that the Croatians would never have encountered a 'greasy surface' before.

When we later discovered that the bloody thing simply doesn't work it was merely added to the list of heartbreaking metaphors that cluttered up the abominable evening. I was transfixed by Bilić – he has menace in his eyes, and in my nervous mind I likened him to an Eastern bloc pimp masquerading as a mini cab operator in Soho. I berated myself for being so racist, whilst my head still hung; ashamed by the comical escapades occurring on the pitch and my own misuse of stereotypes the Croatian fans again brimmed over into their regimented yawp.

Poor Scott Carson looked all daft in his yellow costume. After his initial error, so ludicrous that all present paused to establish that it had actually happened and was not just a big stupid David Copperfield-style illusion before letting the nausea kick in, he became from then on merely some matter filling an outfit standing in a goalmouth. Every time the Croatians surged forwards, mostly on the break, a goal appeared likely and Ivor's remark that England seemed not to have prepared in any way for the specificity of playing Croatia and their ability to inflict punishing counter attacks but simply assumed that a side, already qualified would be happy

Matt Johnstone

for an evening out, was judged to be the most perspicacious of the evening.

Though it received little in the way of competition from me I confined myself to attacking the Croatian team's coats which I judged to be rubbish, particularly in comparison with the rather dapper England attire – in my mind a sartorial competition became the only kind of encounter in which we could triumph.

In the second half David Beckham, dear derided, adored David Beckham offered hope, he knew it was him alone who could offer it. Eighty thousand people scanned the pitch searching for something to be

optimistic about and it wasn't till his arrival that that need found a destination. It was for him alone that I remained to applaud as he left the field, dignified still, saluting the crowd, teased to the precipice of a century. Who knows what will occupy this wasteland when, if he ever surpasses his 99th cap?

McClaren had already sought sanctuary in the dressing room knowing his holiday was already assured along with his severance. Better to be abroad – his umbrella can offer little protection from the current storm.

José makes my day...in another dimension

Having José Mourinho as England manager would almost make up for our failure to qualify for next year's tournament. In a pointlessly constructed parallel European Championship where England qualified one can only assume that we would be attending a competition rife with potential embarrassment and eventual disappointment, although it seems a bit stupid to go to all the bother of manufacturing an alternative reality which is also disappointing so we might just as well imagine one where we triumph.

In fact, I'll be in the team as player-manager, in goal will be Robert Green of West Ham United, Morrissey will partner me up front and at half-time of our opening game (at Upton Park) Daniel Craig and Lindsey Dawn McKenzie will do a live sex show.

'I bet if you went out with Mourinho he'd never call back when you wanted him to, he'd flirt with other people and sometimes just broodily stare off into the distance'

The FA's decision to appoint a 'world-class' manager is a good one but makes me wonder what the previous paradigm might've been. A 'jittery' manager? A 'malleable' manager? A 'nice' manager? The manager of a team of millionaire athletes needs to be big. And preferably swarthy. When was the last time England had a manager with even an ounce of 'swarth'? McClaren if confronted with swarth would piddle. Sven was chic but at the last World Cup Big Phil Scolari's low-swinging sack of swarth sent his tackle on an inward flight. Keegan, Hoddle, Taylor, Robson, all lovely in their way but compared to a gent with Mourinho's obvious sass unlikely to scorch the retina.

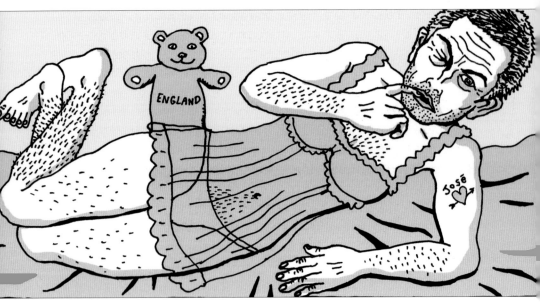

Neil Fox

I've been dying for an opportunity to like Mourinho ever since he entered the English game but his position at the Bridge meant mine remained a secret and shameful affection. I squirmed like Humbert Humbert when he announced his own and Barcelona's teams a day before their infamous Camp Nou clash – 'Oooh he's such a dirty tinker.' Mind games and arrogance are an intriguing and beguiling brew, even from the manager of a detested rival club.

If he were to be appointed it would legitimise my interest, like a knicker thief suddenly made manager of a launderette my prurience would be seen as diligence – 'I was merely sniffing to see if the Lenor had worked.' The position requires a substantial character. One can only truly love someone if they exist to some degree outside the sphere of your control; if in a relationship you can dominate someone completely how can they offer salvation? How can they place their self between you and death?

I bet if you went out with Mourinho he'd never call back when you wanted him to, he'd flirt with other people and sometimes just broodily stare off into the distance and when you asked what was wrong say 'Nothing' – all moodily. McClaren would bring you breakfast in bed wearing a novelty pinny. The England team would have to respect José, he'd demand it and whilst I suspect there was some breakdown in his relationship with senior Chelsea players towards the end of his tenure that, in my opinion, is because he was sabotaged.

That wouldn't happen at England. Sir Trevor Brooking will do a wonderful job in the meantime as a caretaker, he was marvellous at West Ham; revealing unimagined inner wrath on the touchline, it was like seeing a deputy headmaster gobbing at Hell's Angels.

I think the FA should do whatever it takes to get Mourinho, not just because of my silly crush but because I think he could galvanise our crestfallen nation. He could handle the press, the players, the ever-shifting tactical requirements and I don't think we're in any position to quibble about flamboyant football, what we need is success.

It'll be a drag watching events in Austria and Switzerland next year while the English game thumbs its impotent crutch but knowing that José was at the foot of the bed in a baby doll nightie would make the process seem almost tantalising.

Barwick must
atone for the sins
of his fathers

Brian Clough, for all his extraordinary achievements as a player and a manager, is still often remembered as the best manager England never had. I am reading Duncan Hamilton's *Provided You Don't Kiss Me*, in which he chronicles 20 years of interviewing Clough whilst, initially, working for a local Nottingham newspaper. I've not yet progressed beyond the early chapters so Clough is still in his prime; virile, volatile, passionate and frequently unreasonable.

What I enjoy most about this beautifully written and tender account of the relationship between a nervous young nit of a provincial reporter and a football genius is the sense of genuine proximity to its subject, so that Clough's obvious flaws seem forgivable and even beguiling, rather than cruel and unbearable.

'Mourinho's future is yet to be written but let's insist that it is strewn with leading Blighty to glory'

In the introduction Hamilton recounts an occasion where, whilst he was still in his teens, Old Big 'Ead viciously coated him off in the home changing room in front of the wet and nude first team, effin' and blindin' with such ferocity that he feared for his safety while Garry Birtles stared embarrassed at his own nude tootsies. The severity was such that Hamilton assumed that his relationship with Nottingham Forest was finished forever. Naturally, within 24 hours, Clough had called instructing him to get to the City Ground at once and that the argument had been a mere trifle.

From what I've read so far this is a wonderful book but I suppose I ought to reserve judgement – perhaps in later chapters Hamilton loses all regard for his work and just scrawls slogans across the page in nail varnish, which would be absurd and not altogether unrewarding. What I can be assured of is that Clough will descend into alcoholism and stay at

David Humphries

Forest for 18 months longer than he should have, which gives even these early episodes a hue of sadness.

I'm a shade too young to have been fully cognisant of goings-on at FA headquarters at the time that Clough ought to have been made national manager, but have strong memories of his enormous and compelling personality. Once, during a non-aggressive pitch invasion, I think after Forest had won an important cup tie, he clipped one of his own supporters round the ear like an aggressive dad. He was a very potent man with an incredible life force and often such characters are sniped at and undermined rather than elevated and celebrated.

In his pomp Clough would've been a marvellous England manager – he vibrated on a plane of consciousness that made him a formidable leader but unnerved administrators. It is widely assumed that the reason he didn't get the job is because the FA didn't think they'd be able to control him – and they probably couldn't have. That's one of the reasons he'd've been bloody good.

If you have not yet guessed that I'm building towards a rather grand fanfare in support of the appointment of José Mourinho then you don't deserve a newspaper and I suggest you take this copy of the *Guardian*, God's newspaper I call it, and thrust it into the palms of an orphan who will be grateful for the nourishment. I think that by appointing Mourinho we can as a nation atone for the criminal neglect of Clough's talent. Mourinho is his natural heir, more than Martin O'Neill, who admittedly played under him, more than any of the potential candidates. Who could be better? Who could inspire a nationwide buzz in the way that the sexy dog smuggler has so effortlessly done? Wenger or Ferguson? Why, they only have one European Cup between them and two full-time jobs.

I read that Brian Barwick, when asked about the likelihood of Mourinho being offered the job, just stared into space and mumbled bizarrely. Well, that's the wrong attitude, no one ever got anywhere by staring into space and mumbling bizarrely except, maybe, Nostradamus, but it is more for his perspicacity that he is admired than his mumbling and staring. Barwick must immediately cease this mumbling and staring and get on the phone and avenge the errors of the past and give us something to feel optimistic about.

Mourinho's future is yet to be written but let's insist that it is strewn with leading Blighty to glory. Let's as a nation embrace unique and gifted individuals rather than suspiciously eyeing them as they subdue unspent ambition with toxic, bottled anaesthetic.

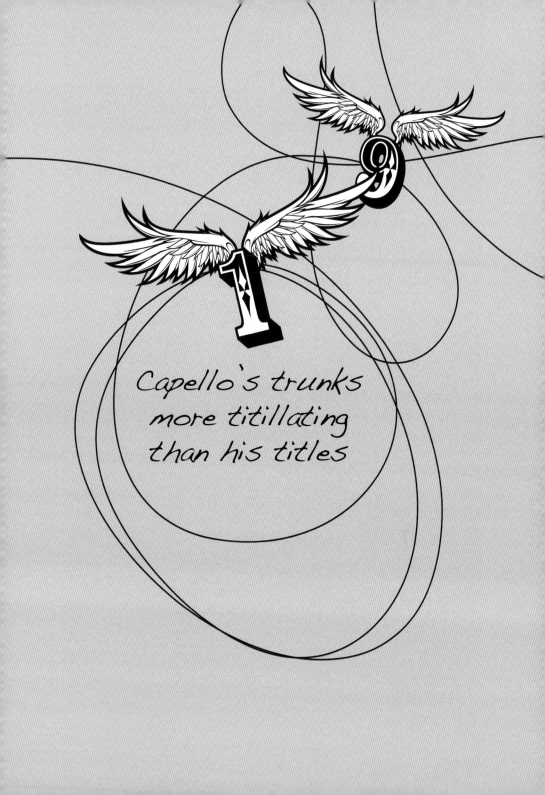

Capello's trunks more titillating than his titles

I suppose my feelings about the FA's failure to appoint José Mourinho exposes me as a rather shallow man influenced by the media, hyperbole and sexual charisma. Of course Mourinho is an exceptional coach but my interest in him being the national manager was enhanced dramatically by the convenient legitimisation that the appointment would've given my prurient interest.

I'm trying to get into the spirit of Fabio Capello's coronation but in spite of his incredible success he isn't a titillating choice. Whilst reading about his triumphs across Europe, the facts with which we are all now familiar, having received a crash course as a nation – nine titles at four clubs, one European Cup, he likes the art of Kandinsky and Chagall – made little impression. In fact I was much more interested in the photo of him as a youth diving into the sea.

Ah, the power of the image. He can top as many leagues as he likes and devour modern art with the rapacity of a Shoreditch fire but unless I get a snap of him in his trunks he can eff off. I was aware of Capello as a successful coach of Milan then as an opponent to David Beckham in Castilla. He said Beckham would never again play in the white shirt – people are always saying that to Beckham, he should work for Daz; no matter how much mud people sling at him he turns up a few days later in a pristine white top and saves the world. I hope the Ku Klux Klan don't learn of his abilities, they'll make him a grand wizard and the unity for which we've all toiled will go right down the plughole as racism is suddenly made to seem fun.

'I would query the rationale of promoting a product with an image so arresting the subject becomes irrelevant'

Them briefs he had on were pretty spick and span an' all. With my easily stirred devotion to image he can count himself fortunate that I don't embark on a campaign to have his gorgeous knob made England boss; him sat there all seductive and reclined, his goolies bunched up into a taut smurf hat between his thighs. I think the ad is for the pants but I would query the rationale of promoting a product with an image so arresting that the subject of the advert becomes irrelevant. When I see that ad I don't think 'Oooh, I must get myself some pants' I think 'Oooh, I wonder if I'm gay.' I'd never wear them pants, I'd feel the pants would be judging me – 'Well these balls certainly aren't golden, they'd be lucky to get a bronze.'

Capello for most of us is as untarnished as David's ballbag; a blank canvas upon which sharp lines of success can be etched or vague, blurred draws and losses can be rendered. When I first see a beautiful

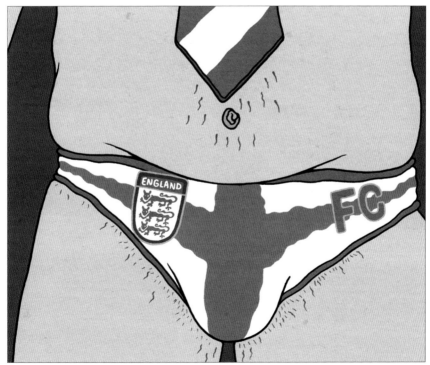

Matt Johnstone

woman my mind floods with expectation and I project a future onto her perfect form; 'She could be salvation, a secular saint, the answer to my murmured prayers' then we embark on a journey that can only lead to disappointment just as certainly as the agonising euphoria of birth is death's first klaxon.

What will we and our red-topped spokespeople make of this apparently educated and brilliant man? Will he be Fabio-lous or Crappello? I no longer care that he's not English – the idea of an English manager being a prerequisite was ground into the dirt like a dog-end with kid's knickers in its garage by the God-awful period under Steve McClaren.

Only Paul Ince seems bothered saying 'it's a damning endikement of our game' or something but given Ince's 'previous' around ties and loyalty – turning up in a United top after making all manner of oaths and pledges to a future at West Ham – we can rinse his comments down the same lavvy my childhood love of him was bitterly flushed.

It's going to be a little while before any of this matters with a barren few years for England but in the Premiership we have an enthralling weekend ahead of us – West Ham will avenge their midweek defeat when Everton come to Upton Park today and tomorrow the 'big four' are all at it in an incestuous riot of money and hype.

Plus Joe Cole came and saw me do stand-up the other night, a man who left the Boleyn with his head held high and his integrity unblemished. So let's not get too worked up about Capello for a while, let's lose ourselves in the national game and use the holidays as an opportunity to ask some pretty searching questions about latent homosexuality. Merry Christmas.

Interview between Russell Brand and James Corden

RB: Do you think Zola is going to be good for West Ham?

JC: I do, I do. It's funny, I looked at some West Ham message boards last night and I saw these fans were saying, 'He's only using the club as a stepping stone to manage Chelsea.'

RB: Mmm.

JC: And I kind of thought, if he comes and manages our club and in four years' time, three years' time, at any point Chelsea are interested in him to manage their club, he's probably done a really good job for us.

RB: Yeah.

JC: And they're not going to be interested in him if we get relegated or we don't really do anything, so you have to give him the benefit of the doubt and go, well everyone has to have a first job at some point, and yeah he might be brilliant or he might not. I just always think you should be positive until you're shown otherwise. It's odd what's happening at the club because it seems like they just want a coach and not a manager as we've always known it, who's someone who buys the players and is in charge of the absolute running of the whole team. It seems the club are going to buy the players and Zola will coach them. It might be the best thing that's ever happened to us or it might be the worst, nothing is guaranteed in football at all really.

RB: I think that he's a charismatic and likeable figure, Zola.

JC: Mmm.

RB: The Chelsea connection is troubling but it's lovely, he is at least an affable likeable man.

JC: Yeah.

RB: And I think that's a good point you've made … because I'm really fond of the role of the gaffer, the, you know, the Alex Fergusons, these characters that have absolute control. It's sad, the erosion of that office is one of the sad things about football, I think.

JC: Absolutely, yeah, yeah.

RB: I didn't like it at the World Cup when you'd see Bobby Robson and they'd say he's the England coach, no he ain't, they're managers.

JC: Yeah, they're managers. The coach always sounds like he's your PE teacher who coaches the team on a Sunday.

RB: Yeah.

JC: I kind of believe in this, in Trapattoni, er no, not Trapattoni, oh who's the guy?

RB: Nani?

JC: Yeah, Nani, I believe in him, I have a good feeling about him and he worked very closely with Fabio Capello.

RB: Really?

JC: Yeah, ultimately it's about feeling … the ultimate feeling, because the most consistent feeling of being a West Ham fan is that you can't help feel that we squandered so much.

RB: Yeah.

JC: Of course, that great crop of players we had come through, we squandered that, and then things like buying Freddie Ljungberg.

RB: Yeah.

JC: …and then paying to release him, or paying Gary Breen forty grand a week and things like that, it seems that we've just squandered either talent or money.

RB: I always feel being a West Ham fan is like an almost exact paradigm of being an England fan, I mean the constant disappointment.

JC: Yeah.

RB: Always being let down.

JC: Yeah.

RB: Occasional flashes where you get optimistic.

JC: Yeah.

RB: Mates of mine that support Arsenal or United or Chelsea, I think well at least when we're having trouble with England you've fucking got club football, we have the exact same experience, but with club football, oh no!

JC: I go to a lot of games with a really good friend of mine called Gavin, it was him who kind of introduced me to West Ham really, and he said this season he would love us to be in a relegation battle and I said, 'Why?' and he said, 'Well, just 'cos it's exciting.'

RB: Yeah.

JC: And I would rather have excitement than what we had last year, just kind of being mediocre, just mid-table, that sort of safety thing. He said, 'It doesn't really thrill me, the safety of that.' I'm not sure I agree, I mean relegation battles are great if you beat Man United on the last day with a player that you don't legally own, that's great fun.

RB: James, you like me are a gentleman off the television who supports West Ham United. What's it like when you go to matches now that you are famous?

JC: Do you know what, it's kind of quite nice because West Ham fans seem to really like people who are on the telly who support West Ham, do you know what I mean?

RB: Yeah.

JC: They really seem to like it. So people are always positive and nice and just seem to want to have a picture on their camera phone and be very nice and say that they like the show, or say how terrible it is that Matt Horn's character in the show, Gavin, supports Tottenham so blatantly in the show and that's about it, that's all they tend to say really, you know. I never feel like, 'Oooh this isn't very safe.' I tell you the best atmosphere I've ever felt was at an away game at Villa and obviously at an away game you have no choice over where you sit.

RB: Yeah.

JC: I was sat amongst some people who looked like the most brutal and hard-nosed people you've ever seen but I've never felt more safe really. It feels like you're one of them.

RB: Yeah. It's nice to have that. Affinity is good to have, something that is grounding. One of the things I enjoy is being lost in the crowd.

JC: Yeah.

RB: And at half time maybe sign a few programmes or whatever but…

JC: During the game…

RB: Yeah.

JC: It's all about the players on the pitch in that game, and no one ever comes up or things like that during the match. You know you're one of a team really, you know you're just a fan, everyone is. Whether you're in a box or you're in the posh seats or you're in the lower, where I used to sit when I had my season ticket … as soon as it starts and they come out you're just a fan.

RB: I sometimes reflect that it's strange to have spent so much time cultivating individuality only to crave being lost in a crowd.

JC: But isn't that kind of the beauty of football really and being a football fan, because I've thought about it quite a lot when I've gone to matches because I always find it quite strange that that many people part with that much money to watch ninety minutes of what sometimes isn't entertainment.

RB: No.

JC: Do you know what I mean? It's actually quite depressing and demoralising sometimes. And yet everyone still goes and I came to the conclusion it's because everybody ultimately wants to be part of something, or belong to something. It's the perfect thing to belong to because ultimately, it doesn't really matter and yet you can give it all the meaning and purpose and emotion that you want to let out. Your sheer joy and elation or anger or sadness or all these things, but within the safety of a bubble so that actually your life isn't tremendously affected. You can let it affect you how much you want to but you're always in control of that. It's not like losing someone in your family or losing a job, losing a pet.

RB: Yeah.

JC: And yet you can make it matter as much as you want to.

RB: Extreme emotion...

JC: (*Long pause*) Oh hello? Are you there?

RB: Yeah, I'm here James, it's just a bad line.

JC: Shall we crack on? Because I'm going to see Stevie Wonder, so we should crack on as best we can.

RB: Ok.

JC: It's always interesting supporting West Ham, I wonder if it's quite as interesting supporting you know, Middlesborough?

RB: This is an interesting point you've brought up there because the writer Irvine Welsh is an Hibernan ... Hibs fan.

JC: Yeah.

RB: And he believes that secretly all other football fans believe that it would be better to support Hibs. I've always thought that West Ham is a well cool team to support.

JC: Yeah, I've always felt that. It always feels like people like West Ham and like West Ham fans. There's always clubs and fans that don't but on the whole it feels like people respect its history I guess – Bobby Moore and things like that and now players like Rio, Michael Carrick, Joe Cole, Frank Lampard. These are all great things, and just an eternal sort of false optimism or realistic optimism. I remember going to one of the opening games of the season and we won, I think it was the season we went up actually and we beat Blackburn 3–1 and because we'd won by that goal ratio we were top of the League and just hearing all these fans walking to the tube station saying, 'We're gonna win the League' and you felt like ninety percent of them knew this was an ironic song but there were ten percent of them who thought, we've just beaten Blackburn, we're gonna win the League.

RB: *(Laughter)*

JC: There's something really beautiful about that kind of thing, you know.

RB: Yeah, the cockeyed optimism. I think it is an incredibly romantic club to support. I don't think there are many teams now in the Premier League, perhaps Newcastle, that have still got that kind of affinity, that relationship with their fans. Everyone that works for West Ham has got the same accent, this club feel to it.

JC: Shall I just tell you the best thing I ever heard a fan say at a West Ham game?

RB: Go on.

JC: He was sat like two rows behind me and we were having a real nightmare time of it, we were putting crosses in but they were useless, they were terrible, and no one was trying or attacking the ball in the box and he said, 'We need someone like Van Nistelrooy or Ronaldo.'

RB: What an astute observation!

JC: I almost just turned round and said, 'Oh, is that what we need, oh right, we should tell them 'cos I don't think they know that, that would be the thing that we haven't thought of, the world class £25-million-pound footballer, that's what we need, Ronaldo, yes we know but we don't have one.'

RB: Yeah.

JC: You know, what a breakthrough.

RB: Yeah, what a breakthrough.

JC: Yeah, listen, it's so nice to talk to you and call me when you're back, and if I'm around I'd love to go to that Newcastle game.

RB: Brilliant, all right we'll go to that together then mate.

JC: I'd love to, all right.

RB: I'll sort it out.

JC: Look after yourself.

RB: You too, enjoy Stevie Wonder.

Inner sanctums
reveal soul of
Hammers family

After the second of West Ham's listless defeats at the hands of the vindictively efficient Everton I snided my way into the directors' lounge, as I was curious to meet the dignitaries within. Since writing this column I've had incredible access to West Ham players and behind-the-scenes personnel and I must say I've found the place to be reassuringly domestic.

The staff have an unaffected familiarity with each other and most of them have been at the club decades; the shop-floor banter between them could be found in any factory or call centre across these islands. I witnessed Lesley and Barbara behind the bar in the players' lounge discussing with eye-rolling boredom the concern of a trainer who informed them that they ought to avert their eyes, as Lucas Neill was coming through in just a towel.

Lesley: 'I said, "I've got two grown-up sons – he's got nothing under there that's gonna frighten me."'
Barbara: 'Chance'd be a fine thing.'
I heard Ron, whose job I was unable to ascertain, glibly dismissing the heart attack he'd had the previous week while filling a see-through bag with unused chops off the hospitality table.
Lesley: 'Did the doctor tell you to watch what you eat?'
Ron: 'What'da they know?'

For me, exchanges of this nature are as warm and familiar as dozing on my grandad's lap, and far more accessible as he's been dead for 15 years. Just to clarify; I only dozed on his lap as a child, not into my mid-teens, just before his death. A lapful of adolescent drug addict could only exacerbate bowel cancer and anyway I'd long grown out of the habit by then. The white radio-clock he'd received from Ford had long stopped but still it hung on the kitchen wall in Dagenham. A plastic monument to his years of toil, a black-and-white photo of him humbly accepting it was in the adjacent cupboard.

As he lay delirious with death approaching, on the settee, TV on as ever, I watched through tears as he struggled to remember Jimmy

Greaves's name.

'Who's that?' he enquired, peering beyond the screen and into the cosy, hazy past.

'That's Greavsie,' I said, all sad. Bert was a West Ham fan of course, like my Dad, and would've been thrilled at the new privilege I now enjoy, though probably too embarrassed to actually get off on it the way I do. I'm intrigued by hierarchy and a Premiership football club is a fascinating place to observe social strata. First there are the fans, themselves organised into myriad groups; then, in the ground and behind the scenes, security and hospitality and catering; the now sadly defunct Hammerettes; training staff; directors; and, fanfare please, the players. I was titillated by Tony Montana's ascent through the cocaine cartels of Florida and South America in the movie *Scarface*: first he's hanging out with street dealers, then local Mister Big-type characters, before climbing to the top of the power pyramid where corrupt politicians teeter.

'The Lyall and Greenwood dynasties truly had the demeanour of aristocracy, a Cockney monarchy'

My own experiences at Upton Park parallel that exactly; Lesley and Barbara are cut-throat Cuban street dealers, Ron and Danny and Tom from security are local Mister Bigs and at the top of the pyramid are the families of John Lyall and Ron Greenwood. And me, well obviously I'm Tony Montana, strutting around in a white suit with a machine gun and a powdery moustache.

The analogy had broken down long before you were asked to accept me as a cold-hearted, hot-blooded killer; Lesley and Barbara wouldn't last five minutes dealing charlie on a corner in Miami and the respective Lyall and Greenwood dynasties have more in common with the House of

Windsor than that ostentatious tat palace that Tony and his cronies were holed up in. They truly had the demeanour of aristocracy, a Cockney monarchy.

Clearly aware of the duty of legacy, they charmingly introduced me to their children; when Murray, John Lyall's son, said, 'This is my son Charlie. John's grandson,' it was touching. Neil, Ron Greenwood's son, a gentleman like his father, was hospitable and gracious, never betraying for a moment that my nervousness was evident. I met a few members of the current board but wasn't with them long enough to make an assessment of them or their intentions towards the club. But the presence of the club's two most successful and beloved managers' families was heartening.

If the line from this game's inception to the present day can be preserved perhaps we can protect its soul through Ron Greenwood and John Lyall, my Grandad Bert, through Neil and Murray right to Charlie. Not his little brother Scott though. He supports Chelsea.

Paddy Molloy

1

2

*Watching Arsenal,
thinking of Sting
and Trudie*

Two thousand and eight then. We're now so far into the future that Kubrick's space vision looks like a turgid and unambitious 'what the butler saw'. I suffered a bit of football fatigue over the holidays as well as that vomiting craze that swept the nation like jacks or pogs – or saying 'whaaasssuuuup' but with such commitment that the utterance becomes projectile.

I feel personally aggrieved by Liverpool's failure to stay with the pace. I really thought this might be their year; to kids growing up now the Reds will be like United were when I was a lad – a team for whom there is an incomprehensible reverence that have never delivered a title in their lifetime. I suppose they have at least triumphed in the watered-down, hyped-up Champions League but the Scousers demand domestic success from their side and now it increasingly seems that will not be under Benítez.

'Matt apologised as if Arsenal's dominance were bad manners and he'd failed in his duty as a host'

I did not go to Upton Park for West Ham's magnificent victory against Manchester United and was in fact so delirious with my Scrooge 'flu that I was oblivious to the event until baffled and congratulatory texts began to flood in. I was at the Emirates on New Year's Day, however, where the Hammers played like a side who felt like they'd done enough work for two matches in their previous encounter – which is a mentality I often employ sexually after the euphoria of the debut has reached its giddy climax, often secretly making eye contact with my cat as my co-participant ponders the whereabouts of the former shaman who now half-heartedly writhes, more for exercise than pleasure.

Arsenal move with the fluidity, grace and purpose of a couple who remain very much in love, the kind of yogic coitus that I like to think Sting and Trudie Styler have. Arsenal pass confidently from deep positions and are unencumbered by needless flair but make the functional aesthetically titillating – again, how I imagine Sting and Trudie.

I don't want to give the impression that I give undue attention to the private lovemaking of Gordon Sumner and his missus, it's just a convenient analogy. I've never pondered it alone, biting my lower lip, eyes rolling skyward as I twitch out ribbons of guilty glee. I don't put on that 'fields of barley' record and pretend to be him while canoodling with a

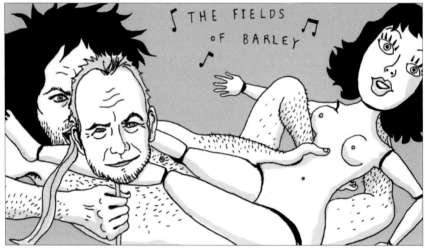

Neil Fox

porcelain sex doll. I don't think you can even get porcelain sex dolls, which is a prohibition of choice that will, surely, ultimately lead to the collapse of consumerism as the anaesthetic of the West.

I went to the Arsenal game with lifelong Gooner Matt Lucas. I don't often attend away games and even as we approached the magnificent arena the angst of unfamiliarity was all about me. The people drinking outside the pubs on the Blackstock Road were not of my fraternity; lacking there was the bonhomie of the frequently defeated, replaced instead by a peculiar sense of assurance; men louchely swilled back booze safe in the knowledge that they were not about to witness a bout of lazy humiliation.

It was a world away from the gallows goodwill of Green Street where a lunatic pervasion of detached joy prevails; revellers indifferently jig and swirl, regardless of the likelihood of 90 minutes of torture, like a grinning gin-bleached hag merrily giving suck to a stiff blue tot.

When Arsenal scored twice, so quickly that the whistle's echo could still be detected, Matt apologised as if Arsenal's dominance were bad manners and he'd failed in his duty as a host. I assured him that he couldn't be held responsible for his team's superiority and spent the rest of the game admiring the architecture and listening to the away support's relentlessly amusing chants with fellow Hammer and companion that day James Corden.

My favourite was 'sit down if you love Tottenham' – there is little standing at the Emirates so by the song's clever logic the home fans were tacitly supporting their hated foes. Their riposte was quite good – 'You need more foreigners' – but all were united in the minute's silence that preceded the match to mark the sad death of Motherwell's captain, Phil O'Donnell, a reminder that, whilst pithy, Shankly's maxim was ever an empty witticism.

22

Don't let Harry
head north
for shooting
practice

I'm on the Isle of Wight caught up in the seductive nostalgia of umpteen childhood jaunts, avoiding paparazzi (two of them, the same two – I can see how Britney Spears has got entangled with one, the proximity begins to feel like intimacy; I almost invited one of them into my bath this morning out of a combination of curiosity and pity) and to tell you the truth nobody reminded me to write this article until moments before the deadline when I was off shooting clays with my chums.

Ah, the power of the establishment. Whilst you may deride it and attack it from the foothills prior to ascent, on arrival at the summit it is very difficult to eschew the baubles and the Barbour. That is why the revolution will be tricky – it takes great discipline not to check your principles at the door of the Groucho and allow your ideals to be neutered by piña coladas and fellatio.

Big Sam Allardyce became the eighth casualty of a particularly bloodthirsty season. I don't recall so many managers having fallen so early on before and Sam was remarkably philosophical, saying there's little point in bitterness or regret in these situations and that's true, but it must be challenging to stifle those instincts regardless of the pay-off.

'Allardyce was vulnerable as soon as Ashley took over but they do seem a bit trigger-happy on Tyneside'

He was ever Freddy Shepherd's appointment so I suppose he was vulnerable as soon as Mike Ashley took over but they do seem a bit trigger-happy up on Tyneside; if I'd behaved with such profligate abandon whilst cracking off clay pigeons I'd've felled two photographers and perhaps an instructor to boot as opposed to the breathtaking displays of marksmanship that have led to me becoming something of a local hero and, possibly, if the legislation can get through before the ferry departs, mayor. All power ought to be wielded in a considered and responsible manner.

Allardyce surely deserved a season, but I suppose if you own a football club that you've loved since childhood and are not happy with the fashion in which it's being run you must act. Like in a marriage, though that's not an analogy that I can personally validate so perhaps, more reasonably, a holiday.

If you go on holiday with a lover and after the first night you realise that you, in point of fact, despise your companion; the way they eat, address

David Humphries

waiters and are cruel to the street cats of Lindos, perhaps it's prudent to give them the old heave ho' and try your luck with a chamber maid. Or in this case Harry Redknapp.

I've said before in this column that I love Harry, I think he was great at West Ham and has done wonderful work at Portsmouth but most importantly he is the most amusing manager working in top-flight football.

Once, on *Goals on Sunday* where he guested with Paul Merson he told an anecdote of Merson's early career at Fratton Park and the special attention granted to gifted players. As is well publicised, Merson had

problems with addiction relating to gambling and alcohol and during one traumatic period he requested some time off to go to Tony Adams's addiction clinic.

Harry consented acknowledging that Merson would benefit from the treatment. When Redknapp relayed this story on telly he went: 'Merse came to me saying can I have some time off to go to Tony's clinic cos I'm having a bit of trouble with the booze, the gambling and the birds . . .' Merson interrupted here, saying: 'Not the birds Harry, I was still married then, remember?'

Harry cared not a jot that his candour had retrospectively devalued Merson's marriage and blithely ignored his former charge's appealing looks. 'Anyway I give him the time off then I got a phone call from a mate, saying "I'm in Barbados, I've just seen Paul Merson on the beach." I goes "No. Merson's in Tony Adams's clinic" – turns out he was lying but he came back the next week and scored twice.'

The upbeat ending of the yarn was somewhat lost on Merson as he was now just staring blankly into camera having been off-handedly outed as a philanderer in a story meant to illustrate his wayward talent.

Some say Redknapp deserves a big stage on which to display his under-appreciated skill. But he is adored at Pompey and will be forever loved in East London and, whilst Newcastle are a fantastic club with incredible supporters, I don't think their administrators deserve a great manager like Harry.

If Keegan's a
messiah I want
the Cockney
Moses

The Dionysian versus the Apollonian, romanticism versus pragmatism, forever we oscillate and vie between these two contrasting ideas. A wise man once remarked to me that the Third Reich was an example of what happens when you put an artist in a position of power; although many of Hitler's atrocities were committed as a result of him being a right bastard as opposed to an artist – there's nothing in pointillism that suggests that genocide would be worthwhile.

I suppose what he was saying was that a personality whose mind is

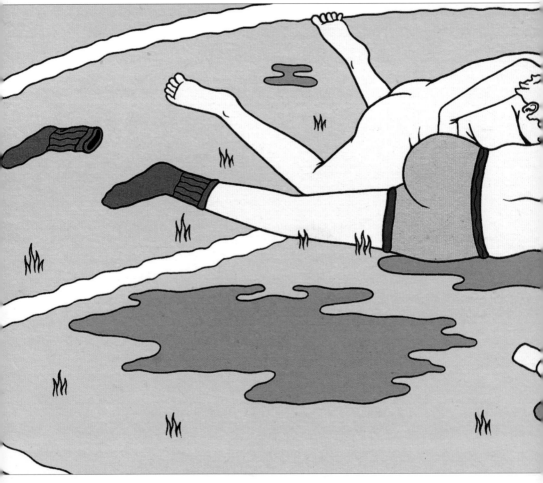

Matt Johnstone

governed by poetic ideas like Bavarian myth and the operas of Wagner oughtn't be put in charge of foreign policy and defence because they'll pursue impractical objectives to achieve, in this case misguided, romantic ends.

Kevin Keegan's reappointment as Geordie messiah made me reflect on this theory. Now, I'm right behind any second coming, it appeals to me, a Geordie messiah, why stop there? Let's have Harry Redknapp as a Cockney Moses and Martin O'Neill as an Ulster Herod. I am enthralled by

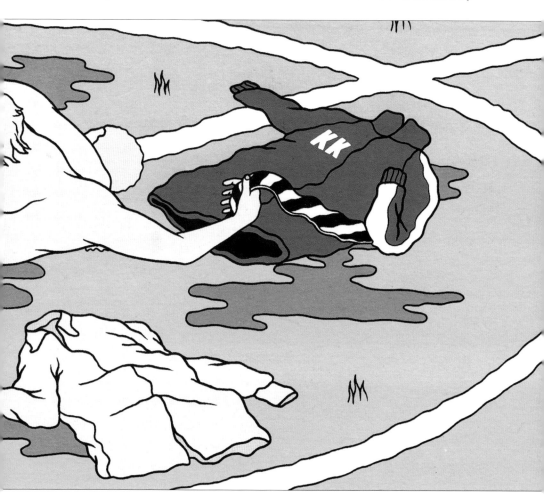

narrative and Keegan's return is a great story; he's an intriguing character who, I gather, is a little embittered about the way he's been handled by the English press and feels he has scores to settle.

I was initially baffled when I heard the news but on reflection it makes perfect sense particularly if regarded as an insular romance between the people of Newcastle and Keegan rather than a managerial decision made by a massive franchise. Because logically, surely, this doesn't add up. When Keegan took Toon on its euphoric romp from the foot of Division One to the summit of the Premier League the footballing landscape was very different. Newcastle were loaded and had few rivals in terms of spending power; that, coupled with Kev's then-untarnished ebullience, was sufficient to bring them tantalisingly close to glory.

'Perhaps it's not for us to understand the Geordies and their rose-tinted fetish of the miner's son'

But if you look at the top flight now can one really envisage Keegan outsmarting teams bossed by David Moyes, Juande Ramos, Mark Hughes, not to mention the big four and Cockney Moses and Ulster Herod? I suppose when you're in love such things cease to be relevant.

'He's got a suspect temperament.' 'Oh I know but look at his hair.' 'He struggles tactically with defence.' 'Yeah, but when he looks into my eyes I feel like I'm the only person on earth.' 'He makes emotional decisions then walks away when he feels the heat.' 'Look, just fuck off will you, I love him.'

For Newcastle fans those fêted few seasons under Keegan still have the power of transcendental love, an idyllic holiday away from the glum drudgery of under-achievement and of course they will once more be guaranteed cavalier, adventurous football – he is the anti-Allardyce.

Perhaps it's not for us to try to understand the Geordies and their rose-tinted fetish of the admittedly adorable miner's son – few outside of east London will appreciate the adulation felt for 'vicious-looking' Julian Dicks, and Robbie Fowler could probably push an old lady in a wheelchair into the Mersey without relinquishing his status as 'God'.

In a sport increasingly compromised for capitalist ends perhaps we should celebrate this tiny triumph of the heart over the head, while Liverpool's beloved Rafael Benítez looks like he's about to be 'Jolled' good and proper by a board that clearly don't respect the feelings of the Kop. The Toon army is being heard.

To me it seems that Keegan can but fail, but what the bloody hell do I know, I'm no expert and I don't support Newcastle but as a fan of football and romance I should be cock-a-hoop at this recalcitrant disregard for reason.

Perhaps Alan Shearer will join as his no.2; they could commence each home match with a *Women in Love*-style nude wrestle in the centre circle while Michael Owen blows cocaine into their anuses. Why not? It'll be a bonding experience like no other.

Keegan's appointment is romantic rather than pragmatic but does that make it wrong? I suppose the correct answer is 'who cares?' It's made thousands of people incredibly happy and unless he's had a massive change in philosophical direction in the interim period the consequences are unlikely to be as horrifically profound as Hitler's elevation. Just to be clear: Keegan good, Hitler bad.

Is Morrissey talking the language of West Ham?

Is it insanely narcissistic for me to contemplate that Morrissey is trying to communicate with me through the wearing of replica West Ham tops? The answer is, of course, 'Yes'. 'Yes it is. Why would you even need to ask?' Well, because I've been courting Morrissey, of whom I'm a lifelong fan (if that life is about 18 years), for several months with the intention of persuading him to commit to a documentary where I interview him, follow him about and analyse his legacy.

'I became rigid with dashed expectation as I awaited my name like it was the sixth Lotto Thunderball number'

He is aware of my devotion to the Hammers and seems rather fond of me; recently on stage at a handful of gigs that I was unfortunately unable to attend he introduced the members of his band before saying 'and I'm Russell Brand'. When I heard tell of this I became all queasy and loopy and reckoned it to be the start of a beautiful friendship with a beloved icon. The knowledge of this name-check dramatically impaired my enjoyment of the performance I attended at the Camden Roundhouse this week ('I don't perform, seals perform … unfortunately') as between each song I became rigid with dashed expectation as I awaited the utterance of my name like it was the sixth Lotto Thunderball number. The trepidation was so torturously unbearable that I nearly leapt to my feet and screeched: 'I'm Russell and I need you to love me.'

Thankfully I just sat there all spurned, listening to the hardcore chant, to the tune of ''Ere We Go', 'Morrissey, Morrissey, Morrissey'. I once did a gig with Noel Gallagher and the similarity between the crowd there and at football was startling but I suppose somehow natural because of the

obvious corollary of those two demographics, but would you expect to find a large terrace fraternity at a Morrissey gig?

I suppose I'm an unlikely member of both groups; alas on that occasion, unlike at Upton Park, I was unwilling to subjugate my identity into the throng but instead perched on my seat's edge wringing my clammy fists like a meekly loyal housekeeper waiting to be listed in the Oscar acceptance speech of an oblivious employer.

At the point in his set where he introduced his band I became so agitated with futile hope that I kicked over my neighbour's drink and locked hands with my companion so tightly that to escape she had to chew through her own wrist like a trapped fox. The fantastic set concluded, quite rightly, without any mention of my name, which has helped me to re-evaluate my expectations of live entertainment. I won't on Wednesday, for

Paddy Molloy

Liverpool's visit to West Ham, expect Dean Ashton and Mark Noble to come out at half-time and sing 'To All The Girls I've Loved Before' without once breaking eye contact with me, and I think that alone will make it a more enjoyable evening.

So, with my unrealistic, egocentric dementia happily acknowledged we can return to the question posed at this article's genesis. On the cover of his new single 'That's How People Grow Up' Morrissey is wearing a West Ham Boys' Club T-shirt – now he did once wear the same shirt nine years ago, before we met, before he would've had any awareness of my existence, unless he was a secret attendant of Grays School's production of *Bugsy Malone* in which I dazzled as Fat Sam, but is there even the remotest possibility that his renewed interest in the garment could've been sparked by my own allegiance to the club? 'No, let it go.' Well, after the show I asked him. Not outright like Paxman, more opaque and obtuse, like Columbo.

I had him cornered but not isolated; also present were the former QPR striker, now with MK Dons, Kevin Gallen and a bloke called Liam, who I think was a Millwall fan. I cagily asked Morrissey why he had taken to wearing the claret and blue, fingers crossed in pockets that the response would come 'Because of you, darling boy' but before Morrissey spoke Kevin said to him, 'You're a QPR fan ain't ya?' and Liam said, 'I thought you liked Millwall?'

I saw this as a brilliant opportunity to recount an intriguing anecdote I once heard on the History Channel, told by an old German man who had once been a member of the Hitler Youth. (I know this is the second consecutive week that I've mentioned Hitler, I'm not secretly Nazi, I don't know why it keeps happening, I think he was a wicked, wicked man. Wicked as in bad, not hip and edgy.)

It was along the lines of: 'We the assembled ranks of the Hitler Youth were watching the Führer give a speech, and at the point he said "You young men are the future of the Fatherland" he looked right into my eyes and I knew he was speaking specifically to me. When I told the other members of my experience each of them said "No, when he said that he looked into my eyes."'

Now I related this to demonstrate amusingly that all three of us had keenly believed that Morrissey was a follower of our chosen team but midway through I remembered *NME* coating him off and calling him racist.

To be clear Morrissey is not racist, and only a twit could make such an accusation. None the less I thought 'Oh no, he's gonna think I'm comparing him to Hitler' – I mean he's a vegetarian, artistic and very charismatic but it's not a comparison I imagine he'd welcome. I began to flounder and back-pedal, trying to distance myself from my words even as they tumbled from my mouth, clarifying and mitigating like a drowning Hugh Grant. When I finished blathering Morrissey gave a world-weary sigh and turned to the other two gents – 'Of course … this is what Russell does for a living' he said.

Well done stern
Fabio for defying
our emotions

Sentiment is adjudged by some 'the unearned emotion' – to mawkishly coo about some cute tot or bumbling pensioner whilst not having to wipe their bottoms or tolerate their gurgling. Hemingway said of his father: 'He was a sentimental man and like most sentimental people he was also very cruel.'

This I understand as the slick transition between snuggling up to an adorable kitten, stroking its fluffy bonce, going 'Aaah. Aaaah. AaaaAaAaaah' till eventually you love it so much that only crushing its skull

Neil Fox

and feasting on its gooey brains will be a sufficient expression of that feeling. I used to cuddle my dog Topsy too hard and sometimes I want to kiss babies with such vigour that my childless status is a blessing to infanticide statistics.

Fabio Capello is neither sentimental nor cruel; he is, on the evidence of his decision not to select David Beckham, and his trophy-spangled CV, a football manager making choices informed by football realities.

Dear old Steve McClaren was like a beige moth flitted about on the farts and grunts of public opinion and media flatulence: 'You don't want Beckham? He's gone. No Paul Robinson you say? He's history. You want

Beckham back? One moment, I'll pop off and get him.' I think we, as a nation, could've tricked him into fielding a team of players' wives in their bras, which I'd've been well into, especially now Cheryl Cole is on the rebound – she may've gone crackers during a goal celebration and leapt into the crowd like a cross between Cantona and Caligula and noshed off them twerps in that brass band.

'99 is an ice cream with a Flake in it. Delicious. What's 100? Just a lousy letter from the Queen'

Capello will not allow his squad to become emotional pornography where we squint and jostle through Beckham's century, teary eyed by the achievement of a goal that is in fact abstract. I believe it was Lee and Herring that pointed out that the only reason we fetishise the number 10 is because we have 10 fingers and if we inhabited a planet of Dave Allens, where everyone had nine and a half fingers, we'd all be salivating at the prospect of Beckham achieving 95 caps, which he's already done.

Although Capello has stressed that the door remains open to Beckham so he may yet acquire the cosmically meaningless accolade of 100 caps, I think he ought be contented with 99. Nine, I seem to remember from my poxy school days, is a magic number, doing all sorts of arithme-tricks and 99 is a type of ice cream with a Flake in it. Delicious. What's 100? Just a lousy letter from the Queen, which I imagine is standardised and just says something like: 'Well done for not dying, love the Queen.' I'd rather have a Flake.

The general consensus throughout the media seems to be that Capello has made the right decision, many applauding his bravery and urging him to go further by axing Michael Owen. Wouldn't it be even braver to immediately implement my excellent footballers' wives scheme where on

Wednesday we'd see a flock of gorgeous harpies tottering out onto the hallowed turf? Plus I'm going to the Switzerland match and I might get myself a kazoo and sit with them oompah pah pah nerds and wait for Cheryl to go nuts.

Hey, I'm not making light of their situation, Ashley is a silly sausage but we all make mistakes – having a wife that beautiful might eventually make you go a bit stir crazy, like being chained to a Canaletto, he probably needed to break out and leer over a Rolf Harris as a kind of sorbet to rinse away the relentless glory of his wife's fizzog.

Some seem agitated that Capello's squad held few surprises, well he does have to pick from the rather limited genre of English footballers so there was always going to be an air of predictability about it. He can't say, 'Up front is King Herod partnering Ray Winstone and in goal is Taylor Coleridge's The Ancient Mariner. Oh no – that's a disaster, he only stoppeth one in three.'

I've seen Capello's Hasselhoff-Grandma face at every football match I've watched on telly so he must have a fair idea of what's going on and I think he's got the right blend of experienced players and Aston Villa treasures. I'd like to have seen caps for Dean Ashton and Robert Green and maybe even Mark Noble but at least I don't have to spend the next few days worrying that they'll have their legs smashed in by England's reckless training methods.

What do they do there? Cage-fighting? I think it's an auspicious start for Fabio; perhaps Beckham will win his ultimately pointless century in a competitive game and we can all have a saucy emo-toss over something that matters.

26

Let's revolt
against Lucre-
more's ludicracy

I'm in Antigua in the Caribbean inhaling limitless beauty and enjoying the unstudied benevolence of the people who live here. Fred, a friendly bloke who works at the hotel and laughs at me or with me – I hope it's the latter, it doesn't do to be presumptuous – took me and my young consort to watch the Caribbean Twenty20 cricket tournament currently in full swing on the island. Cricket is obviously very popular here and this new variation on the formula has taken the West Indies by storm.

I don't know much about cricket; my knowledge was mostly gleaned from a BBC drama called *Bodyline*, which recounted the Douglas Jardine versus Donald Bradman Ashes series, which must've been in the early 30s. Good it was. The trick was to throw the ball at the batsman instead of the wicket, which really spiced things up and I think it ought be reinstated nowadays or perhaps bowlers should be given pistols and shoot batsmen as soon as the match starts making the game even shorter, which I think would be a blessing.

'They want to make as much money as possible whilst not actually appearing to be living incarnations of Satan'

The other thing I know about cricket is from them adverts where Ian Botham and Allan Lamb advertise chops because both their names have 'meat' connotations – Beefy Botham and, well, lamb. The whole silly business made my vegetarianism seem all the more brilliant. The two of 'em scoffing down lumps of flesh, fat and rind between their gnashers going all rancid made me think meat is not only murder – it's also halitosis.

This Twenty20 caper was a pleasant enough evening mostly because of the jubilant carnival conducted throughout the match (Dominica versus Barbados) – often the celebrations were entirely divorced from the on-pitch action. I saw one group of women gleefully gyrate and high-five

David Humphries

when Barbados got 'a four' and then repeat the ecstatic ritual when the same batsman was bowled out minutes later.

This tournament was devised by a Texan businessman who himself had little knowledge of cricket. He owns the stadium and the TV rights as well as having a lot of other commercial interests on the island. Clearly this man had motivations outside of altruism, business people always do. It's how they define themselves – 'Hello, I'm a businessman.' They say.

This globe-trotting soccer circus proposed by Richard Scudamore (I'm suggesting Lucre-more, if anyone wants it, they must credit me) damned by Harry Redknapp as 'unnatural' and Gareth Southgate as an 'April fool' is another decision by the Premier League that does not have the interest of fans at heart. This is not surprising though is it? They are, once more, business people. They want to make as much money as possible whilst not actually appearing to be living incarnations of Satan. It must be a constant exercise in brinkmanship.

The idea of introducing 10 more games decided at random, with the exception that five top seeds will avoid each other, as Lucre-more points out 'imbalances symmetry' as if he's a graphic designer and the fixture list is a logo for a firm of masseuses who specialise in oily hand-jobs.

It's not that the idea is inherently evil, people in Beijing or Sydney or whatever would get the thrill of live English football, which is nice for them. I suppose what is offensive is that this idea exposes the naked commercialism that drives 'our' national game. Which may soon not be exclusively 'our' national game because Reading versus Bolton will be held on the seabed of the Cape of Good Hope.

Ultimately, though, this is not football's problem; we live in a consumer capitalist society, look out your window – that's consumer capitalism out there, as far as the eye can see. If it annoys you then we'll have to have a revolution, which I'm well up for. It doesn't matter if Hillary wins or Obama or McCain so let's stop getting excited about people's genitals, pigmentation and age; they are all tools of the consumer capitalist system that we tolerate and endorse with our apathy.

It will only get worse, they will always want more money, it's the nature of the beast, except it's not a beast, it's a machine, a machine designed to take our money and shut our mouths. The other day I was offered a million quid to do a car commercial, I turned it down because I know that once you take that money they own you.

One could argue that by working for this paper or British TV or companies like Universal I'm already compromised and that's indubitably true. But this is the context we all live in and presently fundamentalism is beyond me. The possibility for change however is perpetual; they can change the Premier League but we can change the world. As long as corporately owned sports are elevated to carnivals by the people that attend them we have hope.

2 7

Potassium-
rich fruit has
no place in
football

I'm off to Los Angeles for a while to make a film and I feel drenched in nostalgia. The cat has delayed further the writing of this piece, which had already been put off to provide a barrier in the form of an English work commitment to curtail the Atlantic's inevitable lure, by lying on my stomach, perfect somehow, peaceful, a living shrine to serenity. Perhaps the pang we feel when we depart from a person or place (or cat) we love is so profound because it is a rehearsal for the ultimate departure, that we will all one day make, unto death.

Intoxicated by nostalgia, United of Manchester were unable to commemorate the anniversary of the Munich tragedy with a victory though in many ways defeat is perhaps a more fitting tribute to such a painful loss. City deserved the win from what I gleaned from a TV screen in an Antiguan suite, where the unusual grandeur of the occasion was heightened yet more by my situation and the period kits worn by both sides.

'I know young folk will think I'm lying but it happened, I was there. We all took bananas to football'

I wonder if the kits affected performance? I wonder if Cristiano Ronaldo's game was subdued by self-consciousness? Or even itchy socks? I know that if I'm wearing new shoes I can think of little else, not through discomfort but through vanity. I might pretend to be listening to an inquiring aunt or potential wife but actually all I'm thinking is, 'I've got these shoes on. Look at my shoes. Notice them. Come on.'

Perhaps Ronaldo was unable to penetrate City's five-man midfield and austere defence not because of their tactics and concentration but because he thought he looked brilliant in his 50s re-enactment costume. Far more likely, of course, that the absence of Wayne Rooney (a man born

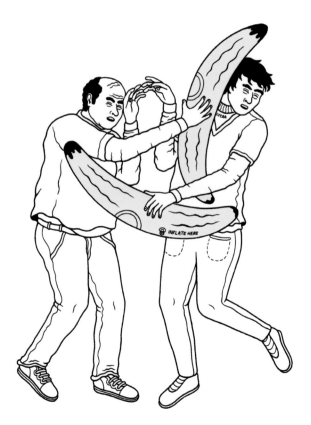

Matt Johnstone

to play football in period outfits – I bet he'd look good as a mead-drinking friar an' all) and the sadness of the occasion affected him.

I see everyone's taken to wearing those vests under their shirts now. Tightly fitted, exact-same-colour-as-the-club-shirt vests. When did this sartorial shift become de rigueur? Who's selling them? They must be coining it in, everyone's wearing them. We've gone from no one wearing them to everyone wearing them almost overnight, like if tomorrow when you left the house everyone you met, literally everyone, had a plastic bra on over their coat. I suppose that would be less rational as these vests provide warmth and the bras would only provide titillation – and only in a few cases. A lot of people would look silly.

The only historical precedent for this seismic yet preposterous cultural shift was that brief, bizarre season – I think in the late 80s – when suddenly, apropos of nothing, everyone at football matches, again, literally everyone, was required to bring a giant inflatable banana. I know that sounds absurd and young folk will think I'm lying but it happened, I was there. We all took bananas to football.

There is no obvious link between the potassium-rich fruit and the game of football. None. Why did this happen? Why wasn't it stopped sooner? I suppose it was harmless fun and may have contributed to the decline in terrace violence as a heated altercation that involves an inflatable banana would look like a confrontation from *Some Mothers Do 'Ave 'Em*.

So last Sunday the weight of history proved too great a burden for the world's best footballer to bear proving that for all their wealth and glamour the modern player does still have a soul. It's difficult for us to get behind young Ronaldo (why are there so many good footballers with variants of this name? Ronaldo. Ronaldinho. Other Ronaldo – who, incidentally should have his hair cut, by force if necessary, he looks like an exotic bumpkin with it long) what with the wink during the World Cup, his incredible skill and most irritatingly his beauty. He's tall and fit and muscly and young and handsome and rich and good at football; why, who could dislike such a character?

I also suspect that he may be no slouch when it comes to picking up girls for no-strings sex. Often I myself feature in red-top tabloids charged with this but let me assure you, should you care, that I endured years of famine in that domain and sacrificed my life and my sanity before my luck changed while Ronaldo did keepy-ups in his pants.

I will miss English football and I'll miss England, a beautiful country that gave the world the beautiful game and rightly we're proud of it and we ought to preserve something of the game's integrity 50 years after an incarnation of the game's joy and vivacity was lost while travelling. I'm glad that the country's Premier League will be forced not to go global.

Interview between Russell Brand and Noel Gallagher

RB: What do you think about the take-over of Man City?

NG: Well, it was really weird judging it from afar because obviously whoever's done the first press release has gone a bit mad and gone, 'We're gonna win the League next year and then we're gonna win the Champions League the year after that, we're gonna buy all these players for this amount of money', and it's like, oh fucking don't say that. Especially for the City fans who were going to see them away to York ten years ago, you won't find anyone that's taking it this seriously – 'Oh yeah, we're gonna win the Champions League with Ronaldo', it's just, 'Fucking hell, we're gonna see some good players'.

RB: I suppose the fact that they delivered Robinho so quickly, it's, 'Oh my God, it's not just talk', because there has been a few clubs where they've been 'Oh we're gonna do this, we're gonna do that' and then actually it just doesn't materialise.

NG: They must've sold it to him on the premise that there were gonna be all these players that were going to come. I mean, you can bid for these players all you want but trying to get 'em to come and live in Manchester … say for instance you're Kaká and you're going to sign one

big contract at the end of your career and it's the chance to live in London for five years or the chance to live in Manchester for five years. Let's say City outbid on the wages and he gets 180 grand a week, I guess you'd much rather live in London, wouldn't you? If you come from Milan. The best thing I heard about the Robinho sale was Pelé saying 'Who? Man City? He must need counselling.'

RB: *(Laughter)* Mark Hughes handled that well, Mark Hughes went, 'It's a shame he's not still playing, because we could've had him.'

NG: He looked a bit shell-shocked on the telly from what I've seen from abroad on BBC World. I just hope they don't force all these players on him and then sack him for not being able to mould this team together, do you know what I mean? Here's these fifteen greatest players in the world, make them all play together or we're gonna fire you.

RB: That's why I think Mourinho was good for Chelsea because he didn't't allow it to overwhelm his overall vision, he was able to go, 'No, no, I don't want them.'

NG: I think he ultimately got sacked for not playing Shevchenko, didn't he?

RB: Yeah, it was only when that went wrong that it fucked up that experiment.

NG: I think if the owners of the club have got anything about them they'll realise that outside of getting Mourinho or Capello, which they'll probably get in a couple of years anyway, then there's no point in getting rid of Mark Hughes.

RB: He's a good, proven manager, it's a different climate for him.

NG: I would say this though, he needs to win a trophy either this season or next season to appease the owners.

RB: Do you think expectations of fans will be reasonable?

NG: I think City fans are different you know, we're not Newcastle fans who think that as soon as Kevin Keegan walks through the door they're gonna win the League. I've known loads of City fans from up there and down here and they're just treating it like a bit of a laugh. The only people who are taking the take-over of Man City seriously are Man United fans. The City fans aren't taking it seriously at all, it's like 'What, some idiot's gonna spend all that money on our club? Bring it on.' And all United fans I know are texting every two minutes. When City got beat by Chelsea I had like 10 texts off of United fans, 'Oh, was that the sound of the bubble bursting? You're not gonna fucking win the League now'. I don't fucking give a shit.

We'll have solid gold goal posts by the end of next season and that'll do me.

RB: Yeah, it really has affected my mate Nik, you know he's a Man United fan and he's going, 'Oh they're gonna have to stop now because they're having a laugh, they're coming across as well arrogant'.. I said, 'Oh no, saying they're gonna buy Ronaldo for £138 million, it's just gonna make them unpopular.'

NG: Yeah, but United have been buying the League to a certain extent, they bought it all the way through the nineties.

RB: Yeah, like Pallister and Ince…

NG: …like Ferdinand. If there was anyone up for sale … they went for Gazza and Shearer and Michael Owen, obviously they didn't do it to the extent of Chelsea, who went and bought a team over two seasons but they always bought the most expensive player, they always had the record signing. So I don't know what they're banging on about but they're taking it really seriously and I think you'll find the City fans aren't taking it seriously at all.

RB: Right, yeah, it's just an enjoyable thing.

NG: It's like Arsène Wenger said, well why don't we get 20 trillionaires in the League, there's still only one trophy. We can't all be in the Champions League. There's only two teams that are vulnerable which are Liverpool and Arsenal because United and

Chelsea are so far down the line with money you can't oust them so you've still got to beat Liverpool and Arsenal. So there's all this, 'We're gonna win the League, we're gonna win this,' that's not guaranteed. It guarantees some decent players and that's it.

RB: Some people think it has a negative impact on the game in general, oligarchs and trillionaires taking over football clubs. Do you think that changes the essence of the game, does that affect you as a football fan or bother you at all?

NG: Well, I tell you what's funny right, is when it was English businessmen who were making millions out of corporate boxes it was never bad for the game. Then when they were taking it away from the working man it wasn't bad for the game. When it was English businessmen who decided that they were gonna stop letting kids in for free nobody said it was bad for the game. But now it's foreigners, it's fucking bad for the game, do you know what I mean? They only care because they're not making as much money, it's been bad for the game for the last twenty years, you know, the corporate side of the game.

RB: Because of Sky?

NG: I don't think because of Sky … I think Sky's made the game more accessible to kids. But I mean the fact that when I was on the dole going to see City, if you brought your unemployment card you got in for half price, that is such a mad idea now … If you turned up at Chelsea with a UB40 and they'd go, 'Fuck off, you haven't got a job.' But that's how football clubs survived. But then with all the money coming in they've put executive boxes in and the grounds are half empty but they can still run their clubs. The likes of Peter Ridsdale or Ken Bates doing it, that's somehow acceptable, but because it's a guy in a fucking turban, it's fucking out of order and they're ruining our game. Well you sold it to these guys in the first place. There are debates about whether it's bad but when they say it's bad for the game, what does that mean? It'll turn fans away? Prices turn fans away. If you want to watch Chelsea it's £75.

RB: I've always thought that just like the world is changing, football is part of the world, the world is more commercial and corporate so of course the most popular sport in the world is going to become more commercialised. It's ridiculous to just say, 'Oh, football's become this thing,' because look at the fucking world, look at the whole world.

NG: There's all that argument about foreigners invading the game and it's bad for the England team. And it's like, hang on a minute the last time I looked, England were always shit even in the eighties when there was no foreigners in the League, they were fucking rubbish then and they're rubbish now. I don't recall England winning any trophies at all apart from the World Cup at Wembley, which a Russian aided the fucking score to. So to suddenly say it's fucking wrong that Chelsea put out a team full of foreigners, well it's full of Europeans, you can't stop that.

RB: We talked about what it was like being at Maine Road when you were signing on … what did it mean to your identity, to be a Man City fan and how has it changed as your life has changed as Oasis blew up and you became famous?

NG: The reason I support City is because they are my local team and you could see the floodlights in my bedroom, and even when we couldn't afford to go to matches, or were too young we'd listen to it on the radio and see the floodlights on a Wednesday night and it was kind of magical, you know. Piccadilly Radio on listening to the match and knowing it was going on just over there. They were my local team, if I'd have lived nearer to United I'd have been a United fan. That was how it was back in those days. How it's changed is I used to stand and sit on the terraces but it's impossible because you're constantly signing autographs for people and you don't really get to enjoy the game, that's the only thing that's changed really. And I guess, the football when you're on the dole, it's the most important thing there is because you've got fuck all else. Your whole life revolves around the football matches, but then once Oasis took off it's a more enjoyable thing, you know I kind of

find it funny when City get beaten. People are very intense about their football clubs and it's because they've got fuck all else. They work in shitty jobs, they married the local bird before she turned fat down the local pub and they've got fucking ridiculous children and to them the *(adopts Geordie accent)* 'Toon is everything man! Me whole life's ruined because of King Kev.' Fuck off!

RB: I saw some bloke yesterday and he was going, 'We'll get 'em taken over and then we'll just get Kev back.' You can't just get Kevin back.

NG: I saw this woman on *Match of the Day* and she had a big placard saying 'Bring Back Kev!'. It was on *Match of the Day 2* and she was going *(Geordie accent)* 'Oh, since the notice has come through man, my whole life's been ruined' and there was a guy kind of stood beside her just going, 'I just don't know what to do, my life's ruined.' What, because Kevin Keegan has quit the football club? Who fucking cares!

RB: Yeah, how could they not know that that was absolutely inevitable, that it was just a ridiculous stopgap employment to distract from all the nonsense going on behind the scenes. He made a lot of mistakes, like that Ashley sitting in the crowd wearing that tigger fucking strip.

NG: Well in one photograph … it's like some of the people from the hierarchy of the other club cease to take him seriously and are just like well, you're just a fucking fat idiot downing pints in one, when really you should be trying to be an ambassador for Newcastle United. And the fans won't take you seriously because they can see through all that. You know the new owners are gonna turn up at City in City kits and all that shit, you go along with it because it's a laugh but you can see through it.

RB: Do you think it's a bit mad that they're called something like Abu Dhabi United Consortium or something? They've got United in their name.

NG: You know I think the whole thing is ludicrous – it's just beautiful lunacy, whereas the takeover of Liverpool, Liverpool have been willing to be bought out by this group from Dubai for the last six months because their take-over's gone mad, and the richest family in the world have just wafted fucking thirty miles up the road, to say, 'Here you are here's all the money in the world.' They've gone from being owned by the Hood, to the richest fucking Arab in the world.

RB: What's it been like, your journey? For me personally it's really mad – I've gone to see West Ham with my dad when I was up to see him at weekends since I was five or six years old and then I'd go with mates when I was a teenager and then I'd go on my own when I was a bit older. It was mental getting famous and then suddenly that thing when you're not just anonymous and suddenly that becomes the focus of attention, but then you get to meet players and have dinner with the chairman.

NG: I remember when City got promoted to the Premier League when Keegan was in charge. After the game they took us into the boardroom and my mate – nobody – just a guy I've known from Manchester all my life, happens to be with me and they were celebrating winning the League and I said 'Can me mate come?' and within twenty minutes they're showing us the plans for the new stadium and he's just some scallywag from Manchester and they're there with a big knitting needle showing us where this is going to be and we're going, 'Yeah, that's fucking brilliant'… but it's mad that you become a focal point and every time something used to go wrong people would shout 'Fucking go on Noel, sort it out'. What am I gonna do you know? Fucking sort it out! I'm like, 'Right, yeah, I'll write a song, that'll inspire them, yeah.' When they were in the third division, we were at the lowest of the low, I remember going to see them play Wycombe Wanderers away on a Tuesday night, fucking shit it was, one nil down after an hour, it was freezing cold with the City fans going, 'Come on Noel, get your fucking hand in your pocket, sort it out!' And I remember going, 'I've got £175. That's all I've got on me, enough to get a decent pair of boots, that's it. "Fucking sort it out, Noel, come on!" What do you want me to do, go in and fire the club? I'm a supporter like you are.' But you become this focal point for all their frustration, and all me mates are going like 'I'm fucking sick of this, Noel why don't you buy the fucking club?'

RB: One of the things that has changed a lot in my life is the idea of having something that's the same, that's good, I've still got that.

NG: That's what's the great thing about football, that's why people don't understand it's the greatest sport in the world, it's all the teams – not like in American football, when they call a team a franchise that they can move to whatever city they want. They can play in Oakland or they can just move the stadium to wherever they want to because they've got no local fan base as such. People from Dallas support the New England Patriots because they're the best team last year, whereas with all football clubs all over the world they're all part of the community and no matter what situation you're in, the one constant thing in your life is looking for the football results. Which is why football is such a special thing because it's all part of the community.

RB: It's pretty mad to think that your journey went from looking at the floodlights at Maine Road through your bedroom window to meeting the players and them showing you the plans for the new stadium.

NG: The journey is the middle bit, Oasis playing at Maine Road – fucking mental you know. When they said you had a chance of playing Maine Road it's amazing

to think that you were taken there as a four-year-old boy who was like, 'Oh yeah, fucking wow,' and then growing up there and throwing coins at all the fans and all that, and then you end up standing back of the terraces, and then you're making your way to the fucking boardroom. Because for a while we were bigger than Man City so when we went there it was a major fucking deal, you were brought out onto the pitch. Whereas if you were a Man United fan when you're a celebrity it didn't wash there 'cos Man United were bigger than anything.

RB: Writing that column in a way I get good access to West Ham now, and so say you'd see a game and you'd think that wasn't a very good performance, but you'd know you were going to meet them later. I can't go, 'Fucking hell, what a ridiculous display, you played shit', or 'He's put on weight, should be playing with his heart on his sleeve'. You'd think, I'm gonna meet him behind the scenes.

NG: Well, you can't speak objectively. When it all went tits up at City for Stuart Pearce, I'd already met him and he's a great guy. And people would say, 'What the fuck's going on at City, it's fucking awful,' and I'd go 'Yeah … he'll get it right,' and you just want to go, 'Oh that's fucking useless, what a load of shit that is,' but because they know who you are, you can't. It's usually when things are going wrong you'll get the call from Five Live saying 'What's going on at Man City?'

RB: The first time they ever let me on the pitch I was just sort of there hanging about and when you thought about it everything was abstract. When you're watching it and you're part of 30,000 people or whatever, and then when you're famous you get level pegging with them.

NG: But don't you find that once you've been brought in to the other side you start talking in those clichés where you never actually say anything. 'What do you think of Alan Curbishley?' *(Cockney accent)* 'I think given time he's gonna get it right you know, I think it's a tough job and you've got to let 'em bed in and all that.' I think given time you start talking in those clichés.

RB: 'What do you think about Frankie Zola? You know he's an inspirational player at Chelsea and…'

NG: You turn into a pundit because you know everything you say is going to get written up, whereas if you're just a fan you can just say it like it is.

RB: He shouldn't be at fucking West Ham, he's got no experience! Italy play negative, that's the only experience he's got, it's against West Ham's nature.

NG: I'll give him six weeks.

RB: It'll be over! 'Cos the reality is with anything like that if West Ham lose eight or ten consecutive games, what are they gonna do? I know Steve Clark has joined him and Mourinho really rates Clarke and he's been at Chelsea under three managers…

NG: I think with West Ham … the managers never seem to be the problem, it's the overall running of the club. It's not the fans because the fans are fucking brilliant, they had the greatest manager in the world in Harry Redknapp and if they'd have kept him what a team they'd have now. It just seems there's always a kneejerk reaction to a minor problem, it's the same with City, I think for the likes of Curbishley to quit anyway, I think he was looking for a way out because a real manager wouldn't just fucking quit and go public and say, 'They wouldn't let me run the fucking club how I wanted but I'll put up with it because I'm a professional.' Whereas Keegan and Curbishley were very quick to say, 'Right I'm off, bye!'

RB: *(Laughter)* You know Irvine Welsh, the *Trainspotting* writer said this very interesting thing. He supports Hibs and he's always secretly believed that other fans think Hibs is the best club and are jealous and want to support Hibs. Not that they are saying Hibs is the best club but that there's something cool. And I've always thought that a bit, you can support Liverpool or United or Arsenal or Chelsea or Spurs but I've always thought there's something about being a West Ham fan that's somehow cool, it's East London.

NG: I think only West Ham fans and Man

City fans think that. We always have this thing in Manchester where all United fans somehow they were all juniors within the young City Fans Club from when you were like three to a teenager, called the Junior Blues, we always said, 'Oh they're all fucking Junior Blues,' you see, like Manny, they all went to City first then they changed. But it's only City fans and West Ham fans that think, 'Oh we don't need the trophies, 'cos we're cool as fuck.' And the reality is, I'd trade a little bit of cool for one tiny little trophy.

RB: You'd trade a bit of cool for one trophy? West Ham were 4–0 against City! And City scored twice in the last ten minutes, the West Ham fans were doing a conga, just oblivious!

NG: When Man City were in the old third division and then when they were in the Championship, Maine Road had sold out every week, the worse it got, the more people came. That mentality is mental, that blackness, 'I'm not going, no I'm not going, I need extreme shitness before I go and watch that club.' The stadium was only full for the first time this year on Saturday because Robinho was playing.

RB: What is that, what is that mentality? Is it representative of something? I saw this thing once when West Ham played Liverpool at the Cup Final a few years back. I went with my mate Adie and he's in a wheelchair and we were in the disabled section. There was this dad there with this

lad who was in a wheelchair and this bloke was a proper hard West Ham fan and this lad was frozen with cerebral palsy in a wheelchair. And the dad was getting more and more agitated over the course of the game and I noticed that most of his vitriol and raging was reserved for the referee, he'd go 'Oh, referee, it's not fair, it's not fucking fair,' and I started to realise as I started to romantically conjure up in my head that he'd always wanted his lad to be a footballer and to be a West Ham fan and some unfair authority figure, God or whatever, had meant that his kid was in a wheelchair and so he vented most at the referee, 'It's not fair, it shouldn't be like this.' He was just a man standing next to his kid in a wheelchair going 'It's not fair, it's not fucking fair,' and I thought, 'Wow, for him this represents the unfairness of his life.'

I think that quality is a consistent thing no matter how much money you give it, or how much the players cost, or how many European players are in the team: it is made consistent in that it is something that is representative of your life.

NG: West Ham would be one of those clubs where you'd think if they get relegated it really wouldn't fucking matter. Whereas for Newcastle it would be devastating, they go on about the Geordie Nation and all that, but you check back and see how much the crowds were down. But you think for West Ham they'd still all go there because I think West Ham fans and City fans have this romantic notion that everyone that supports the club lives within 500 yards of the club. Even when we go abroad we meet a foreign City fan and it'll be like *(American accent)* 'Oh, my Dad supported them,' yeah, well why do you support them, what's it gotta do with you? You know, you're not from Manchester, you have to be from Manchester to support them, 'Oh Man City, Man City rule!!!'

RB: I've been going to football a few times when it's a season like, 'Oh yeah, we're gonna get relegated, no no we'll still turn it around,' and then it turns into, 'We're definitely gonna get relegated,' and it's a turning point of acceptance, or, 'At least we'll see them win some games,' and it's like we look on the bright side.

NG: That's it. Every time City got relegated we'll think, at least we'll get to the play-offs then we'll get to Wembley!

RB: Now what about England, I know that Frank Skinner believes that he supports England but it's a working-class preserve to have an affinity to a club, that it's more middle class and indicative of the way that football has changed to follow England. I know that a lot of people who support Mansfield or whatever and smaller clubs will give a lot of affection to England to have a bigger thing.

NG: I don't think you can pin it down to one kind of group in society. There are toffs that go, you know Mick Jagger and all

that, then the middle classes that go and then the out-and-out fucking thugs that go, the racists … it's just a nice cross section of this beautiful country that I live in…
To me, if you support Mansfield or if you support Halifax they're not going to win fuck all, but you won't support Man United, won't fucking support Liverpool 'cos they're not your local team, the next thing is England. I've got a feeling that when the players are getting booed, like Frank Lampard, it's by Derby Country fans or Halifax fans because they're used to watching local lads you know. 'Honest fucking football and that cunt there's earning 80 grand a week.' I don't think you'll see an Arsenal supporter who watches the Premier League every week give a big boo to Frank Lampard or Beckham. That's all these fat-head fucking Northerners who come from fucking Burnley.
I think the England thing is quite weird because I've been to lots of England matches and you're always sat beside a different person every time you go. It's more of a family thing with England. But it's strange to think how England are seen by the rest of the world. I went to the World Cup in Germany and it's almost like this circus coming to town and doing interviews with German television in this bar and you're on live German television. And er they're going *(jovial German accent)* 'Will you be urinating in the street later?' Oh yes, yes.

RB: We're on schedule here, we'll smash up this bar.

NG: 62 minutes, 1–0, prepare to fight, fight! Urinate, then deportation.

RB: So say you could pick and choose, City win the Premiership or England win the World Cup?

NG: Oh, City win the Premiership. The thing that just pisses me off, we were in America when we found out Croatia had been beaten 4–1 and Theo Walcott had scored a hat-trick and it's like when that little girl won that junior tournament at Wimbledon, now she's gonna win five Grand Slams in a row. It's typical of this fucking country, any time that there's any modicum of success it's like, 'We are gonna be the greatest sporting nation in the world,' and as soon as it goes wrong it's, 'They fucked it up for us! We could've been the greatest nation.' Well, hang on a minute, Theo Walcott's not the greatest footballer in the world, that much has been proven already, and you know when it's his next game playing for England he'll be shit. In England we don't do common sense, the press set the tone for everything in this country and fuck me, they cock it up. Theo Walcott, he's the saviour of English football and at this rate we could actually win the next World Cup – we're not gonna win the World Cup, if we get to the fucking semi-final we'll be lucky.

RB: Most likely we'll get to the quarter-finals and then go out. I don't understand that phenomenon at all, because you'd think after doing it so many times experience would tell you after a win like

that, then you go to a major tournament, struggle to qualify then get past a dodgy team in the first round, then go out in the quarter-finals. It's almost like that pattern is so often repeated.

NG: You'd think these football experts that sit round that table on a Sunday morning on Sky Sports debating all sorts of manner of all shit, you'd think that they know that England on paper have a pretty good first eleven and after that you're fucked. So if you've got more than two injuries in that first eleven, we've had it. Because with the best will in the world Jermain Defoe and fucking Jermaine Jenas and all these people. They're not world class. You'd think they'd know that.

RB: Jermaine! We're bringing in the Jermaines, there's Pennant, Defoe and Jenas!

NG: But because they've got fuck all better to talk about and they've got to talk about something. What I can never understand about England is what the lions are all about, there's no lions in England.

RB: There's no lions. *(Laughter)*

NG: There's no lions in England, why are there lions on the badge? They should be called the three seagulls or the three salmon, there's no lions in England.

RB: The indication is of grandiosity, the detachment from reality, we are the lions of England! Where are these lions?

NG: We have three lions at Whipsnade Zoo, three lions. It's all bollocks. I don't know, you see those guys on the television and one minute they're going, 'Fabio Capello he really should learn the fucking language,' the next Sunday they go, 'Well, he says it in his own way.' (*Italian accent*) 'You no good. You're fucking shit, you're not playing.' You're just talking out of your fucking arseholes constantly. Back to the point though, if England won the World Cup, I don't think we could deal with it.

RB: Why, what do you mean?

NG: Well, because anytime an English team wins anything it always seems to be a full stop. They never go on and do it again. Like when the Argentinians and the Germans would win the World Cup and then the European Championships and then defend the World Cup and get to the semi-finals. Every time an English team has won the Ashes or the World Cup or anything it always seems to be, 'That's it, we've done it now,' and we take our foot off the gas and all get on the piss and then they're never heard of again. I don't think English people are ready for a World Cup winning team – everybody would get knighted. *Everybody* would get knighted – anyone who went to that game is gonna receive a knighthood.

RB: Do you think there's something integral to the identity of this country that couldn't handle a victory, like it would be too monumental and contrary to the way

we see ourselves? So like City fans only going when City are losing, so it's like almost as if it's in opposition to how they see themselves?

NG: We actually spoke seriously about this, what would we actually do if they do win the League? And we were like. 'I'm not quite sure how I'd react to that.' I'm more used to just celebrating coming fourth bottom so we live to fight another day. I'm not sure how I'd react to somebody picking up the trophy. I'd be shell-shocked – I wouldn't know how to handle it.

It's like when West Ham got to the cup final and we were saying to West Ham fans, 'Oh, it's going to be great, what are you going to do if you win?' And they were like, 'Well, I don't know.' You all accept before you go there you are going to get beaten by Liverpool, you must've accepted that before you went there. It'll be a great day out, if we score first, brilliant.

RB: It's really weird that you say that, because when we went 2–0 up and at that point I just sort of went, 'Oh no. Oh, come on! Get one back.' And when they scored and it levelled it out a bit it and went into extra time, they're gonna score, they're gonna score', and then Stevie Gerrard scored.

NG: I guess because it's always been this 'thirty years of hurt' and all this shit with the England team and the World Cup, if we actually won it, what would be the point of carrying on after that?

There'd be no point. We'd have won it, we'd have lived to see it, they'd repeat it endlessly on television, they'd all get a knighthood and it would be like right well, what now, we'd have to say England are officially pulling out of football, the quest is now complete.

RB: Right. That's true you know, I see that makes sense. Because the legend of English football needs constant failure to carry on.

NG: Football fans wouldn't know what to do if England were in Johannesburg at the 2010 World Cup Final and won on penalties. They'd be like, 'Well, we'll just get to smashing things up now. What should we do? Do the samba? We don't know what to do here … honk a horn?' You know the England psyche is to get beaten on penalties, preferably by the Germans, or any other country we've gone to war with, you can put Argentina in there. We were at war with those fuckers. I don't think England fans would be able to deal with winning the trophy.

RB: This all makes sense. I realised then that I've probably never thought of it as an actual possibility when you see England go out to Portugal or Germany or in 96 as well, when that happens, that in itself is the fulfilment of your expectations, that is the trophy.

NG: If you close your eyes, it's like with the City thing, if I close my eyes I cannot see

that trophy being lifted by a guy in a sky-blue shirt, I cannot see John Terry holding that trophy up. I just don't fucking see it. The amount of times I've switched off the TV if England have been knocked out and gone, 'I can't wait for the papers in the morning, that's brilliant, like fucking fifty pages, fucking 'kill 'em all'! Portuguese bastards! English bastards! And me missus going, 'You love it and it's better than going "Oh, we won … oh we're in the semi-final, er … we've never been here before, oh, we don't know what to do."' There's the fall out of the game, there's the referees address, there's the violence of the city afterwards, 'We were robbed.'

RB: Effigies burnt.

NG: I prefer all of that. I wouldn't know how to deal with success for England.

RB: And I think that's part of our whole national identity. I don't think that's just you and me, I think that's a country that feels like that.

NG: Well, it's that thing that I've never quite understood, England always likes a gallant loser. And they say that around the world, 'Oh, fair play always does for the English.' But I think somewhere down the line that must be right, that we've never really been able to deal with success.

RB: 'Cos if you're Brazilian or German that's sort of part of you – winning.

NG: Yeah, you know when you put eleven Italians or Germans on a pitch in a tournament, where there's something just clicks that they're gonna fucking win and that's the end of it, unless they play each other, the winner of that is gonna go on and win the World Cup. That's usually the way it works. But with the England team it's like, 'We're gonna get as far as the quarter-finals and then we're gonna get beaten,' and everybody kind of goes, 'England's gonna get beaten, we're gonna smash some stuff up and then we're gonna go home,' and we all know where we stand and we'll all come back in four years and do it again. That's England's role in world football.

RB: That's why I think if you're a West Ham fan or a City fan that is then replicated at club level. You might get to the final, you might have a good cup run, you might avoid narrowly relegation or win the Championship, but you know you're never gonna win the Premier League, that's not gonna happen.

NG: No, of course not.

RB: So it must be weird to be a Man United fan or a Chelsea fan because then on club level you have that experience of victory and winning things and on a national level it's a different thing.

NG: They take the winning of it all really seriously and my old fella said to me once when we were kids and Liverpool won the title eight times in a row or something, and I was saying, 'Why doesn't it happen to Man City?' And he said, 'What, would you rather be a Liverpool fan and knowing you were going to win every week?' And I was like, 'yes … I would actually, you know.'

And once you get older you think, well you've got more to lose really. The kind of the magical journey of the likes of West Ham and City fans of getting to the Cup Final, 'Oh fucking hell, I'd wonder what we'd do if we won.' Like on Saturday, we were watching the game and Robinho gets the free kick and he scores, and you're just thinking, 'Is he actually gonna get a hat-trick? Could that fucker…?' I don't know why, what to do if he has the best game of his life and he scores a hat-trick and we beat Chelsea 3–0 and the papers are all … I wouldn't fucking be able to deal with it. I'm kind of glad we got fucking beat in a way, it's like, yeah we're still Man City.

RB: (*Laughter*) It's like football's representative of something in football fans, something as a person. And if their game changes too much – it don't matter if there's loads of money or loads of European players coming in, if you're a City fan you're always gonna lose, if you're a West Ham fan you'll have a little run, and then England are always going to disappoint you and you need those things to be consistent to provide stability.

NG: There is a stable law of have and have-nots in world football and in British football. I don't think you can change the fact that England sit about fifth or sixth best team in the world always. But for some reason, whether it be the Italians going to that World Cup match fixing, it's a fucking scandal or the fucking chairman getting put away, Juventus have been relegated, but they're going to win the World Cup somehow. You knew they'd fucking win it somehow. The Germans always get to the final, somehow. The Argentinians are always there, and the Dutch play their role as the gallant fucking wizards who always go out just before they should have. Even in European football, no matter how shit Milan are perceived to be or Real Madrid or Barcelona, they are always there. Particularly in our lifetime, apart from Chelsea who've kind of bought it, there's never been a club that's muscled their way in and been a powerhouse in European football. I think it's pre-ordained.

RB: *(Laughter)* It's pre-ordained, it's destiny, it's in your blood.

NG: I never felt I was supporting the wrong club. I think the people that change when they're like seventeen or something, 'Oh you know we used to support Leicester and now we support Man United 'cos, er well…', oh, fuck off. I was born to be in this situation, with this shower of idiots playing this fucking game.

RB: Like the colour of your eyes or your hair, and like at my school it was mostly West Ham fans, one or two Arsenal fans and it just feels right.

NG: I was born to be a City fan, I never chose City because, when my dad was taking me they just happened to be the best team in Europe at the time, they'd just won the UEFA Cup and the FA Cup and the League the year before. But … there it is, big floodlights, that's my team. But I think you'll find Arsenal fans have all got this kind of demeanour about them, they look slightly like they're shit dancers.

Every time Tottenham get to the Cup Final you can't get a taxi for love nor fucking money, seriously, and Chelsea fans some of them can be fucking nasty … the only time I've ever been seriously abused was at Chelsea, not in the ground, outside the ground by 50-year-old fucking fascists. West Ham fans, they range from, well there's yourself, there seems to be a lot of musicians who like West Ham and artistic people who like West Ham, plus there are Ray Winstone types. But I think Arsenal fans are…

RB: You think they'd be shit dancers?

NG: I mean, if you look at them, no chance.

RB: That's brilliant, nice one.
    Who's your favourite ever City player?

NG: I'll probably say Colin Bell, but of the modern era I've gotta say Shaun Wright-Phillips or Ali Benarbia, go Shaun Wright-Phillips because he's fucking little and he means it.

A lament for
Gazza, whose
gift became his
curse

It all looks a bit barmy from here, let me tell you, your country, your customs and national sport. I'm in America making a film and keep up to date in the following ways:

1. The internet, especially the *Guardian* and BBC websites, which as well as providing information act as a kind of spiritual sorbet cleansing my soul after the inevitable porn trawl that occurs whenever a laptop is flipped open.

2. Photocopied English newspapers from a company called Newspaper Direct which, while excellent, do not carry, for reasons incomprehensible to me, my column; meaning I cannot use it as a platform to attack or praise people that enter my life in the most trivial of ways.

3. An invention called 'slingbox' which enables you to access your TV at home through your laptop so you can record *Sunday Supplement* and watch it, as I have just done, on Thursday.

The aforementioned lunacy of your country, England, is further exacerbated by hindsight. In last Sunday's show when discussing Wednesday's Champions League fixtures the assembled journalists – Brian Woolnough, Patrick Barclay, Oliver Holt and Ian Ridley – were still reeling from Liverpool's defeat to Barnsley in the previous day's FA Cup tie and deduced that Internazionale would annihilate the Reds.

'It's been a macabre descent, his ever-juvenile mind racing to keep up with his peculiarly evolved sporting ability'

I watched safe in the knowledge that Liverpool would triumph 2–0 and, might I say, that in spite of the fact I was regarding their predictions retrospectively, I allowed a superior smirk to play upon my lips. 'You poor naive fools – Liverpool will bounce back. Also you might like to avoid the

Neil Fox

Newcastle Malmaison, I sense Gazza might have a turn in there.'

This was one of the stories that led me to conclude that the Isles had gone wild in my absence: Gazza has been sectioned after 'playing up' in a hotel. I hope both he and the hotel are OK – Gazza I adore and I seem to remember that the hotel in question is quite pleasant an' all.

His descent has been macabre, his ever-juvenile mind racing to keep up with his peculiarly evolved sporting ability. When he was the world's best footballer all the tics and gurning and outbursts were an interesting complement. Now, with his gift departed, he has just become an annoying hotel guest. How unfair that his talent could not be reallocated across the narrative of his life so that in times of distress and despair he could whip out a ball and juggle his way through the lobby to freedom – assuming all his transgressions occur in hotels.

Nani looked, for a moment, in Manchester United's Cup match against Arsenal, that he might retain possession, ignore gravity and dash off into the streets. This Gazza-like display of brilliance, far from earning him plaudits, led to chastisement from Arsène Wenger who thought he was showing off and his own manager who also thought it unnecessary.

Well I thought it was terrific, at least the pixellated version of it I witnessed through my laptop was. I don't know why he was scolded for that. The charge appears to be that he was showboating – good. He didn't do it in a ward for terminally ill children, which would be a cruel venue for feats of physical prowess, he did it on a football pitch during a football match, many would say the ideal situation for such an absorbing display. I also enjoyed his scissor-kick, somersault celebration although I'd be the first to condemn him if he did it in a refuge for battered women.

Perhaps one day Nani will have cause to rue the imbalance brought into his life by his talent. In 20 years' time he may find himself alone and broken in a Holiday Inn and have no magical resource with which to hypnotise a disgruntled night manager but I doubt it.

Gascoigne was ever a unique case belonging to a time before footballers became superstar athletes. He had a natural affinity with fans and was so iconic because he seemed like a normal bloke in possession of an unearthly gift. Only in hindsight is it apparent that it was also an unbearable curse.

Congratulations
to Spurs for
their lowly bauble

SPURS ARE RUBBISH!

When you watch a foreign game on TV in England, like Barcelona versus Real Madrid at Camp Nou, it looks a bit odd, there is a filter, a lens. It seems somehow alien and, well, foreign. The noise of the crowd is qualitatively different. The screech, while as loud as usual, through the speakers sounds further away and everything, to quote Coldplay, is all yellow; a contemporary sepia hue.

When we are shown a clip of American news on English telly it too looks abstracted and, again, all yellow. When I watched the Carling Cup Final (other beers are available) it had, perhaps due to my current exile, adopted the appearance of foreign football. Wembley rang out with a shrill San Siro tenor, the commentary was baffling and Jonathan Woodgate looked like he did when you'd see him play for Real – all far away in a headband.

'A dinner lady needed to stroll over to Robbie and offer to hold his hand till his melancholy subsided'

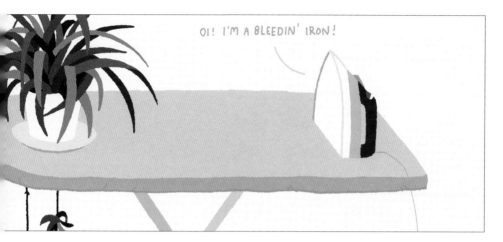

Adrian Johnson

It was confusing to regard the familiar through the eyes of a stranger, like when you come home off holiday and your house seems a bit different and the cat doesn't love you any more. All the more confusing as my friend Nik had mistakenly scheduled our viewing based around east-coast times and when we settled down to watch the game it was already into extra-time.

I don't really approve of Spurs winning anything; they are in fact the only Premier League side I feel innate dislike for. Well perhaps not innate. It is unlikely that the feelings of disdain are inborn and that if by way of some bizarre mix-up I'd been raised in Nepal I still would think, 'Oh they're so arrogant. They aren't a big club. Bill Nic, Blanchflower and Greavsie are names so distantly glorious that they might as well be monikers of Snow White's minions.'

The likely truth of my antipathy is that Tottenham are West Ham's nearest rivals in the misunderstood terms of an ability-meets-geography Venn diagram. Arsenal are too good to get worked up about as, of late, are Chelsea. Fulham don't have the support to appear truly threatening and most other London clubs are an inconsistent top-flight presence so, with the obvious exception of Millwall, the feuds aren't perpetual.

I'm an only child myself but I gather that in large families the siblings that are closest in age are more likely to indulge in conflict – whenever I was frustrated as a lad I had to cook up some spurious quarrel with a spider-plant or an ironing board. It is in this spirit of fraternity towards botanic life and domestic appliances that I'd like to extend my heartfelt congratulations to fans of the Lilywhites. It's been a long time coming but even the lowliest of baubles is preferable to famine.

What's more I did feel chuffed for those present – even through the prism of transatlantic telly their jubilation was evident. As was Robbie Keane's – he did a bit of the ol' crying, always a big plus for me to see a sobbing footballer as it brings them into the sphere of my experience, all teary and puffed out, though with me it was during matches at school playtime not after a cup victory. For the parallel to have been enhanced a dinner lady would've had to stroll over to Robbie and offer to hold his hand till his melancholy subsided.

While the Chelsea vs Spurs final may have lost something in translation, Eduardo da Silva's heartbreaking injury tore through the screen with nauseating clarity. The twisted sock and bone, the anguished referee and Cesc Fàbregas's hands cupped over mouth drinking in his own tender mortality. How do they ever come back from those injuries? Do they? Are they ever the same? At the very least their innocence is lost, and in most cases a yard of pace.

We certainly won't see Eduardo play again for the best part of a year by which time the bilious glare will have faded and championships will have been decided. When Kieron Dyer was injured earlier this season I felt again the grisly pang but I've seldom thought of it since unless selfishly lamenting West Ham's lack of depth in midfield or how useful his pace would be in opening up Chelsea this afternoon but he has lived with it every day.

In a week or so I'll have forgotten about Eduardo so I'll wish him a speedy recovery now and hope that the player that returns has all the skill and grace of the one that fell last Saturday.

30

Is this the right
fertiliser for Grays'
grassroots?

It's all well and good English clubs marauding through Europe winning matches all cocksure and swaggering like it were the barmy ol' days of the Empire once more, strutting through the Champions League knocking over tables in piazzas and laughing at Greek fellas wearing national dress but in Blighty the oft-cited yet frequently neglected 'grassroots' of the game are being bizarrely mishandled.

'I'd worry that I'd tended the roots too aggressively like Steinbeck's Lenny loving another mouse to death'

I suppose the phrase 'grassroots' has caught on as the game is played on a grass surface. I don't much care for the metaphor of tending the 'roots of grass' on my knees with tweezers, forever avoiding worms and worrying that I'd tended the roots too much or too aggressively like Steinbeck's Lenny loving another mouse to death with his clumsy thumb. The only time the game's grassroots are mentioned is in connection with abuse or neglect; e.g. Trevor Brooking'll go 'we must be sure that the game's grassroots are properly nurtured.' You never hear someone say ''Ere, the grassroots are coming on a bundle – thick, lustrous, flourishing things they are, if anything we need to impede the progress of these effin' roots or they'll turn into triffids and devour us all – get some weed-killer.'

The term came to my attention once more this week with the FA's judgment that non-league Grays Athletic FC must pay £14,000 to their former player Ashley Sestanovich who has been convicted with conspiracy to rob and imprisoned for eight years. Grays terminated Sestanovich's contract prior to his conviction but the FA's judgment means that unless they pay the player's wages for the preceding five months they could face suspension from all competitions.

I'm from Grays and spent many happy hours at the Recreation Ground

David Humphries

where the team played their home matches, admittedly mostly on Guy Fawkes night where a lovely firework display took place. The few football matches I attended were bloody dismal, but there is no denying that the games, and fireworks, I saw were taking place on grass and beneath that grass were roots. In short, Grays Athletic are a good example of the game's grassroots. The club chairman, Mike Woodward, has said he will not pay the fine either from his own pocket or the club's resources as a matter of principle.

In addition to being club chairman Woodward is also its owner and manager, a kind of non-league Abramovich minus the marionettes or perhaps more generously a Willy Wonka-style football benefactor. I like that he does so many jobs, I bet he's at the turnstiles taking money then pops on a false moustache, dashes round to the pie stall and knocks out pasties, then darts to the bench in a sheepskin, spraying away the Ginster-pong with a tin of Lynx – he's running that club and furthermore he's single-handedly making a stand against a loopy edict from Soho Square. Apparently Sestanovich, who only had three training sessions at the club and played for 20 minutes in a friendly, initially told officials that he was being held on motoring offences. When they learned he was involved in a robbery in which a man was murdered Grays terminated his contract but because he was arrested after he signed for them the FA say Grays are obliged to honour his contract up until the point of conviction, under contract law.

It's difficult to determine what moral stance one ought rightly to take in such an unusual situation. Until conviction Sestanovich (whose name I'm already sick of typing, I wouldn't have wanted to be the woman in court who had to keep minutes – she must've been writing it constantly on that typewriter with only three buttons. Ghastly) was innocent so entitled to be paid but now he's been found guilty should he receive retrospective payment? Not in my view, it sounds like as well as being a crook he was rubbish. Twenty minutes of match play? Three training sessions? Darren Anderton would've been embarrassed by those statistics and he's never been convicted of conspiracy to rob – he'd've been too poorly to

complete an entire robbery anyway, they'd have to bring him off halfway through.

Also he, SESTANOVICH (I capitalised it to spice his name up) doubled for Thierry Henry in a car ad. What kind of bonkers treble life is he leading? Half-hearted training by day, a quick impression of Henry at lunchtime then cooking up robbery plots in front of the telly at night. Perhaps that's what drew the equally versatile Mike Woodward to him in the first place; he recognised another shape-shifting utility man and snapped him up – the meeting in which SeStAnOvIcH was signed must've resembled a film starring Alec Guinness and Eddie Murphy, each of 'em leaping in an' out of their various identities.

Whilst I acknowledge that the FA has no power to override employment law I think they have an obligation to be supportive to Grays Athletic at this time of crisis, giving them 14 days to pay this fine or risk suspension seems draconian. It is a malevolent gardener who so unthinkingly condemns his lawn. Instead of administering the Baby Bio they're out there blundering about in stilettos.

31

What's the point
in replaying a
humiliation?

If a match is on television that I'm already aware West Ham United have lost I don't bother to watch it. What's the point? The football? What, on their inexorable trudge to defeat the Hammers might do something sexy and skilful? Well, that's great but prior knowledge of an unpleasant result, for me, negates enjoyment. It's difficult enough to watch West Ham live, when the possibility of victory theoretically exists; remove that and all that remains is masochistic snuff soccer.

The way football is televised over here, in Los Angeles, is usually several hours after the event. I've accepted it now. Like many other previously bizarre aspects of their culture, I no longer gawp or even remark, I simply look out the window and get on with my life. Everything is too far apart and crossing the road is illegal. Shops and cafés don't let you use their toilets. In fact nothing that doesn't directly hoover up money from your pants (trousers) is allowed to flourish.

'I'd sooner watch last season's thrilling home defeat to Tottenham than the 4–0 kick in the nuts we got last week'

If I wee'd gold coins Starbucks would let me use their bathroom (lavvy), as it is I spend a lot of my time piddling in the street like a cur. Why, too, are they so euphemistic about bodily function? Restroom? What, for a rest? A rest where faeces emerge from your anus? That's no kind of respite from the trials of the day. Having said that, I've been utterly seduced by all the rhubarb and glamour to the point that when I hear 'West Ham lost 4–0 again' I allow the shame to drizzle past and pop out and buy myself a new bikini. It's my optimism that prevents me from watching a game which I know the Irons have squandered; in spite of irrefutable proof that the result has been decided I sit pointlessly willing alternative results with my brain.

Matt Johnstone

It's stupid enough doing that at a live game, like trying to will Frank Lampard into being sent off or Jermain Defoe into missing a penalty – both of which have happened this season, but surely (surely?) that's not as a result of my mental dexterity and villainous telepathy? I'm pretty sure that once, on acid, I was able to make a weather girl stutter just by staring at her on GMTV thinking 'Stutter, stutter!' but my testimony is perhaps marred by the LSD.

A consequence of my reluctance to torture myself with West Ham's inefficiency and my cynicism has been that I've not seen West Ham play for ages; they seem only capable of humiliating defeats at present and if I know they've lost 4–0 to Spurs I don't see why I should subject myself to 90 minutes of doomed cock-eyed optimism.

Julian Dicks, perhaps the most popular left-back in human history (Roberto Carlos? Kenny Sansom?) has berated West Ham for 'not trying' in recent games, as well he might, for when he played for West Ham it were as if what were at stake was not the abstract idea of three points but the safety of his own sex organs – which were never in jeopardy. It would be a foolhardy pervert who targeted the genitalia of the terminator; I imagine his sperm was a caustic liqueur that would devour the deviant's hand.

Dicks spared Alan Curbishley in his venomous ejaculation, saying he wasn't to blame. Curbishley was also offered support from the board and it comes to something when a vote of confidence is universally accepted as a tacit admission that the manager's days are numbered.

Where else would such loopy double-speak be de rigueur? Maybe in mob culture where the thoughtful and delicious delivery of a bit of fish means one of your mates has been murdered. I suppose at least you've got the fish to cheer you up afterwards – a bit of salmon would take the sting out of all but the most sudden bereavement.

A quick glance in the direction of St James' Park puts Curbishley's recent achievements in perspective. Dear Kevin Keegan seems to be meticulously nurturing a somehow unforeseen travesty for the people of Newcastle who, with the benefit of hindsight and a near certain awareness of the result, appointed a man for whom optimism is the sole qualification.

I expect members of the Toon Army would happily re-watch the games that have taken place since Keegan's appointment, glued to the set, rattle in hand waiting for Bolton Wanderers to capitulate. After last season I suppose mid-table mediocrity is quite an achievement but I miss the adrenaline and adventure. I'd sooner watch last season's thrilling home defeat to Tottenham than the 4–0 kick in the nuts we got last week, because the spirit of the team that game was spellbinding, which I suppose is what Julian Dicks is getting at and why Newcastle are still enchanted by Keegan.

Hurrah for
super, special,
Sunday
soccer-day

It's super soccer Sunday! It's super soccer Sunday! In addition to being Easter (oestrogen? Oh yes, it's all to do with eggs) the celebration of Christ's resurrection and the rebirth of nature itself through the sexiest of the seasons – spring – Manchester United play on-form Liverpool and Chelsea take on the Gunners at the Bridge.

A toy shop round the corner from me in Hampstead has a sign in its window confirming its holiday opening times which reads: Good Friday 10am–3pm, Easter Sunday 10am–3pm, Holy Saturday 10pm–3pm. Holy Saturday? There is no Holy Saturday, it's just Saturday, a Saturday like any other. Holy Saturday sounds like an exclamation made by Robin on discovering that Batman had only recruited him for weekend bumming. However holy Saturday may be in the eyes of Hampstead's toy shop owners, it is as a child's plaything compared to the divinity of Sky Sports' super, special soccer Sunday.

'I think there is only one messiah appearing this Super Soccer Resurrection day and that is Cristiano Ronaldo'

Easter after all yearly shifts, being celebrated in March, February or April as God sees fit – I wouldn't be surprised if suddenly we had to contend with a new Easter 2, 'this time it's personal' turning up mid-June. As a religious festival it is all too capricious, a whimsical affair obeying only the cosmic wandering of the moon. Whereas super, special, sugar-free Sunday special soccer-day is a regulated occasion appearing at the behest of Sky, whenever they deign the event ought to occur.

I wonder if the final match of the season in 1989, when Arsenal beat Liverpool at Anfield to win the title, when Michael Thomas scored the winner, had been prescribed by Sky? Or if the Stanley Matthews final should retrospectively be regarded as the super Stanley soccer final? We'll never truly know. The only thing of which we can be certain is that football matches are now scheduled for the convenience of Sky TV and although, I'm sure, there'll be many negative side effects due to the rise of billionaire media tyrants, one positive we can all take from the monopolisation of our sporting culture is a magnificent day's viewing on Sunday.

Starting with the incomparable *Soccer Supplement* in the morning, a programme so assured of itself that it doesn't even say goodbye at its conclusion but its participants continue chatting as the credits roll, indifferent to our eyes, on to *Goals on Sunday* where we reprise the previous day's events with Chris Kamara and whoever partners him this week after the regrettable departure of Rob McCaffrey, then the main

Paddy Molloy

event – *Super Soccer Sunday*, an alliterative football festival which will pin us all to our couches, grateful for our relentlessly rewarded immobility.

I hope they don't find a way of making Mondays entertaining or before too long we'll be committed to a lifetime of vicarious titillation, whilst the seasons come and go and Easter sprays random festive celebration across the pages of the calendar like an indiscriminate teen onanist decorating Keeley Hazell's paper chest.

Manchester United will win the title this year. They have steeliness to their play and stability that one cannot imagine capitulating. Liverpool squandered the opportunity to end their barren spell by neglecting to capitalise on the remarkable form of Fernando Torres.

Of course, Rafael Benítez can argue that by resting him earlier in the season he has facilitated Torres' recent form, but this I believe to be balderdash.

A friend of mine did some work with Liverpool and told me that Torres is an incredibly serious young man, which is pleasing to me. He's so beautiful and skilful that he could be forgiven if he were giddy and frivolous, forever letting off fire alarms and pinching girls' arses, but apparently he has the demeanour of a young clergyman, poring over scriptures and worrying about his soul.

I think he could've played another 10 games this season and had he done so Liverpool would still be in contention. Arsenal seem now to be tainted by Eduardo's terrible fate and tread the turf as though desecrating his grave, but this is an opportunity for them to turn that around as Avram Grant's Chelsea seem not to have the stomach to overturn first-class opposition.

Reportedly the team has become detached from his leadership and he is seen as a dead man walking, yet if ever there were a time for such a figure to triumph it's Easter. I think there is only one messiah appearing this Super Soccer Resurrection day and that is Cristiano Ronaldo – I think it is he we shall all be worshipping come the festival's close.

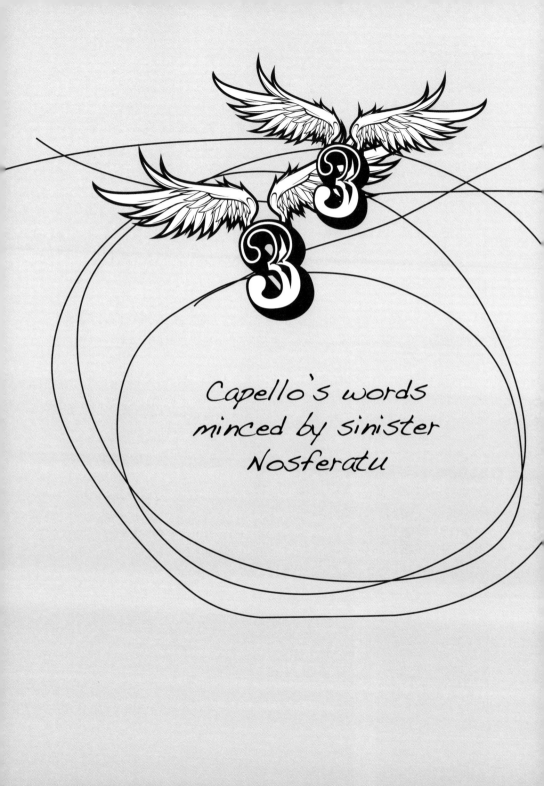

33

Capello's words
minced by sinister
Nosferatu

The pervasive anti-climactic pang that accompanied Wednesday night's defeat in Paris will be present throughout the European Championship this summer so I hope I can learn to love it. The niggling affection of my England support is like scratching a long-amputated limb; did our country ever possess the qualities I lament? A night in Munich? Victory by a single penalty against Argentina? Was Gary Lineker ever more than a snack-grabbing sauce-pot?

"'I am the Maradona of oral sex," claims sweet old man'

This was an especially drab showing, throwing those memories into doubt. Haunted by an extinguished love affair, the memories of distant bliss seem to absurdly mock the tedious present. Fabio Capello seemed pleased enough in his post-match interview; part Nan, part David Hasselhoff, he drily batted back enquiries, often without awaiting translation from the looming, pale translator, played by Bernard Bresslaw as a scheming undertaker.

Ray Wilkins, with the newly depilated Richard Keys in studio, offered an explanation for Capello's ability to respond to questions without awaiting Lurch's interpretation – 'With foreign,' he began, 'you can understand it but you can't speak it.' Personally I can neither speak nor understand foreign but Ray, who played for several years in Capello's Italy, must've been forever confidently nodding at waiters and wailing street widows before drawing them a picture of his response – 'I'll have the sausages' or 'He's gone to a better place.'

Looking at Capello's Munster linguist it was difficult to imagine José Mourinho fulfilling the same function for Bobby Robson at Barcelona. I bet he gave dear Bobby's Spanglish ramblings his own spin; I reckon there are still people in Catalonia who consider Sir Bobby to be a preening narcissist after receiving his persona solely through the Special One's filter –

'"I am the Maradona of oral sex," claims sweet old man' screamed one headline.

Now I don't speak a word of Italian, but I still believe the undead interpreter was editorialising when asked if there was anything positive to be taken from the performance. Amidst all the rolling 'r's' and repressed melodrama I distinctly heard 'Joh Kohl', which I know from my time spent

Paddy Molloy

in Tuscany is Italian for 'Joe Cole'. After Capello had finished, Nosferatu took to the mic but peculiarly neglected to include any mention of the former West Ham hero. Given the nature of the question, we can only assume that Capello had said that Joe Cole's contribution was positive; then, for reasons known only to himself and Bram Stoker, the interpreter omitted any Cole praise, perhaps fancying the nimble midfielder for a latter-day Van Helsing who could at any moment appear in the corridor and plunge a stake into his dark heart.

Aside from his backroom staff of Transylvanian exiles Capello has further bleak characters to ponder. What's eating John Terry? The once strident epitome of English grit, stripped of his captaincy now seems to be castrated and unfocused – perhaps since the departure of the world's most handsome misinterpreter he has lost his way, a conundrum doubtless enhanced by the arrival of Avram Grant, who could easily inhabit the same graveyard utopia as Capello's grim sidekick.

David Beckham clocked up his century, but apart from one cross and a lovely bit of embroidery on his shirt made no impact. Perhaps Capello's instruction to concentrate on crosses was deliberately left untranslated by the Draculian ghoul in charge of communications. I bet everyone's game suffered with him swooping about the dressing room; trying to avoid garlic – not easy in Paris – he must've been a bag of nerves.

England were proper shoddy Wednesday and I feel more disheartened than I can recall by the lack of invention, structure, imagination and flair. To whom do we turn now that Goldenballs' seed can no longer be depended upon? Where do our hopes now rest?

Perhaps we should adopt the policy once favoured by Royalists and consider skipping a generation when electing our next deity – forget Charles and move straight to Wills. Let's not fret further about Shaun Wright-Phillips or Peter Crouch, let us bound merrily to Mark Noble and the incomparable Freddie Sears, whose name ought be eulogised in the form of a parody of The Beatles hit 'I Get By With a Little Help From My Friends' – not 'Billy Shears' as Ringo sang but FrEeEeeDddiEEe SeEAaaRs. And God bless Paul Jewell.

34

My adventures with Beckham in wonderland

David Humphries

I didn't see the Champions League games because I've been spending all my time with child actors, Adam Sandler and a guinea pig – in a professional capacity of course, I've not become a bizarre pervert with remarkable contacts.

Out here in Hollywoodland access to football is limited but proximity to mind-bending glamour is at an all-time high, why, one can scarcely leave the house without being smashed in the face with dirty great lumps of fame. That is why this week's column is jam-packed with genuine scoops, such as you might get from a genuine journalist – unlike a genuine journalist however I have licence to provide as much context as I wish and here it is.

'The conversation may've lasted nine minutes before security prised my jaw from his divine ankle'

On Tuesday night I performed a stand-up show with comedian Greg Proops who you will remember as the Elvis Costello-looking American gent from *Whose Line Is It Anyway?* The crowd of about a hundred people were strewn with stars such as Flight Of The Conchords, Fearne Cotton, Drew Carey, James May (out of *Top Gear* – that threw me), legendary producer Tony Visconti and Colin Hay – the bloke who wrote 'I come from a land down under.' To be there at all was bliss but to perform was very heaven – aside from the plaudits and accolades that dripped from the ceiling like hot wax I was able to check the lyrics from Men at Work's best-loved hit – 'where beer does flow and men chunder' is just one of the evening's revelations; which is a terrible advertisement for the Antipodes.

Afterwards, in the spirit of celebration, I headed off to what can only be described as a swanky karaoke bar, keen to impress all present with a flawless rendition of 'I come from a land down under' without even glancing at the screen. However this breathtaking plan was put aside on arrival to 'The Villa' as there, within its confines, immaculate, impeccable and drinking bottled water sat David Beckham. That's right, David Beckham. Fearne Cotton cannot ever have been so hastily elbowed aside as she was when my hungry eyes met those ever twinkling peepers of dear David.

The next few minutes occurred as if unfurled from a celestial fairground; whirling lights and giddying mist, my hand on a sinewy shoulder, flashing blue eyes and a chuckle like cool water over smooth pebbles – all the while 'A land down under' lulling me into a waking Shangri-La. What follows are the snatched reminiscences of a conversation that may've lasted as long as nine minutes before security prised my jaw from his divine ankle.

Obviously, he's utterly lovely and sweet, this we all know, and my favourite moments from this encounter were these: at one point he said, quite unaggressively and entirely in keeping with the tone of the natter, 'fucking' not as a verb of course, merely for emphasis, I can't absolutely remember the context because of the pounding of my heart but it was something like 'Yeah, LA is a fucking nice place to live.'

Now he's a 32-year-old professional footballer from Essex, swearing oughtn't really draw comment. I suppose it's because we see him speaking on TV so frequently courteously that it was like seeing the Queen apologise for a fart. A further highlight came when we discussed a forthcoming LA Galaxy fixture:

Me: Is it at home?

DB: Yes.

Me: Oh. I'd love to go. Ooh, do you think you can get any tickets?

DB: (with wry curling smile) Yeah I think so mate.

One can hardly imagine a situation where David Beckham would be denied comps for his own side's games; he could probably get tickets to *La Bohème* at Sydney Opera House with a snap of his fingers. How daft of me. Then after apologising for 'talking shop' I asked what he made of the current England set-up and his own fitness and how playing in the MLS will affect his international career.

He said that Fabio Capello is a great manager who was fantastic at Real Madrid and will turn England around efficiently and expertly over the next six months. He said that training and fitness in MLS are as good as in Europe because American sporting technology and ideology is so advanced. And he said that he will keep playing internationally for as long as his legs will carry him.

David Beckham, on the basis of my encounter with him is a charming, intelligent and charismatic man who emanates warmth and star quality in a manner comparable to Princess Diana – for this alone he ought to be kept in the team for as long as he's willing to turn up. And for any who doubt the ability of this extraordinary athlete and ambassador, indeed any who would seek to cross him on or off the pitch, I think Men at Work put it best when they said 'you better run, you better take cover'.

'I hear that some regulars at the Bridge would prefer Chelsea to be knocked out of the Champions League and to drop out of the title race just to be rid of Grant. Astonishing.'

Sorry. Sorry for not doing my article last week. If you were disappointed then I know how you feel, I used to be terribly upset when Jon Ronson's column failed to appear in the Weekend magazine supplement that accompanies this very paper, on one occasion bothering to text him to personally berate him for his absence.

It's not that Tim Dowling, the fella they got in to replace him wasn't any good it's just I felt, and in fact feel, a strong sense of identification with Jon's writing especially when he scribbles from the core of his incessant embarrassment and uses his column to score points in domestic clashes. I still miss his contributions and now only look at Weekend at all because of Dave Shrigley's cartoon – if he leaves I shall simply leave Weekend untouched like the detested Jobs and Money section, too boring even to line the cat's litter tray – he'd become constipated rather than defecate on all those tedious career opportunities.

'I think that I exemplify a common phenomenon in my admission that I put aside my disdain for the Blues whilst Mourinho was at the club'

When José Mourinho left Chelsea he did it in the certain knowledge that he, like Ronson, was irreplaceable. It would've required a manager with the looks of George Clooney, the brain of Richard Dawkins and the charisma of Charles Manson to assuage the sentimental tumult inspired by his departure. I do not like Chelsea but I was sad to see him leave and I think that I exemplify a common phenomenon in my admission that I put aside my disdain for the Blues whilst he was at the club. He made Chelsea palatable.

Figuratively the scenario is reminiscent of a girl I once dated who had an atrocious personality (cruel, racist, joyless) but a really nice arse. She was like her own arse's irritating best mate – I had to tolerate her to get to the arse. The arse in its spellbinding beauty made her many flaws tolerable – she later revealed she'd only gone out with me because she liked my cat so don't feel too sorry for her.

Mourinho was like that girl's beautiful arse – while he was at Chelsea few cared that they played stifling football for a humourless billionaire, we were too busy ogling the arse. Now that gorgeous set of buns has been replaced by the saggy rump that is Avram Grant no one gives a monkey's

Matt Johnstone

that the results are quite impressive, we still mourn the departure of the tanned hide of the Special One – 'I hate it that you're leaving but, boy, do I love to watch you walking away.'

I hear that some regulars at the Bridge would prefer Chelsea to be knocked out of the Champions League and to drop out of the title race just to be rid of Grant. Astonishing. As he himself pointed out, who would've thought when Mourinho wiggled off that Grant would still be in the running for major honours this late on in the season? One suspects that Chelsea will win nothing, naturally. That United will wrap up the title in the next few games and that Liverpool will bounce them out of Europe but none of this matters to Roman Abramovich, who is apparently poised to give Grant a hundred million to reinforce his squad over the summer.

What's going on? Why does that seem so absurd? Why are we so unwilling to accredit Grant? I've a friend who's a season ticket holder in SW6 who swears blind that during matches Steve Clarke and Henk ten Cate conduct tactical powwows, literally, behind Grant's back as if snogging out of sight of an unwanted chaperone. Players are breaking ranks to announce to the press that they never would've joined the club to play for him and more childishly that they call him 'the professor'; not in the way Arsène Wenger is called 'the professor' – affectionately, because of his keen, tactical mind – but because they think he is a right dickhead. A dickhead professor who no one likes.

Didier Drogba is said to be leaving, only delaying his decision on destination until old sweet cheeks has picked a club, and many more, reportedly, will follow. Quentin Crisp said, 'Charisma is the ability to influence without logic', and this is the key to Grant's problem – he can do all the publicity he likes or sit through a press conference issuing only yes or no answers but he'll never manipulate the manner in which he's perceived because he cannot make us put aside logic in the way that Mourinho could. The only thing I can remember from all the press I've read about Grant is that his wife once drank urine on an Israeli TV show. It's gonna take a lot more than that.

3 6

From Bridge to
Boleyn with
Littlejohn on a
limo-bike

I'm going to two Premiership football matches today, like I'm Tord Grip or something, flitting about making shrewd judgements and stroking my Scandinavian chin. I've never attempted such a feat before, many have said it can't be done, but at 12.45pm I shall be at the Bridge (I'm not paying for a ticket and am therefore not contributing to Avram's dopey war chest – in the TV in my brain I always see a pirate's treasure chest when that idiom is used, bulging with rubies and doubloons, though that'd be a fat lot of good in any proper war. On the same dubious basis I refused to buy my friend Les who lives in Los Angeles a Spurs top, even though he'd cherish it and be deeply moved, I just couldn't bear the idea of the revenue ending up in Michael Dawson's trousers.

'There is no decanter, no boomerang-shaped aerial or dividing screen between you and the driver'

Furthermore making any kind of purchase in Lillywhites sports store in central London, where I planned to coerce my friend Nik into conducting the filthy transaction as my emissary, is like trying to score smack in the Kremlin, it was like they didn't want to sell me anything. If we're going to surrender our souls to consumerism we should at least end up with a product. I'm aware this is still in parenthesis and has gone on for too long and that you'll have forgotten the main thrust of the article, don't worry, we'll be back into the primary narrative in a trice) watching the title-deciding clash between Manchester United and Chelsea then I'll be bounding on to a 'limo-bike' and darting off to Upton Park to watch the Hammers take on the Toon.

That may well sound hectic and I imagine it will be, also the term 'limo-bike' may conjure up rather a glamorous contraption in your neuron-box. Well know you this: a 'limo-bike' is a misleading piece of marketing language to inaccurately describe a motorcycle taxi service.

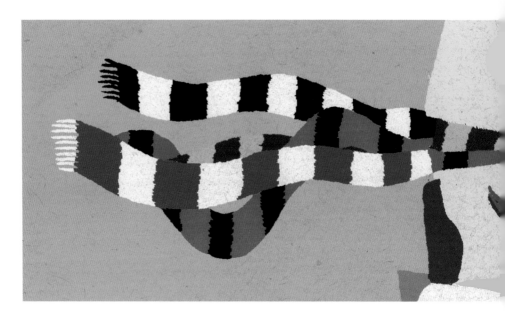

A less disingenuous name would be a 'motorbike' because that's what it is. There is no decanter of sherry, no boomerang-shaped television aerial or dividing screen between you and the driver, in fact you are forced to cling to his waist like one of Fonzie's girlfriends. Also his helmet is wired to your own allowing him to make a one-man radio show broadcast directly into your head, usually covering hot topics like immigration and gays. It's like developing schizophrenia and discovering your louder persona is actually Richard Littlejohn.

I don't usually attend matches as a neutral, for me if West Ham aren't playing I'd sooner watch it on the telly, confidently, in my pants. But Chelsea vs United at this stage of the season will be a spectacle. The last match I went to which I wasn't emotionally involved with was Celtic vs Rangers last season and it was thrilling. The distance and detachment afforded by the removal of loyalty and commitment improved my ability to discern and comment. I became aware of strategy and the use of space.

Adrian Johnson

At Upton Park I'm transported back to my childhood and I witness the fixture from a cradle of emotional turmoil. West Ham's presence disrupts my critical faculties. If I was watching a pornographic film and suddenly my mother appeared on screen, tipsy in a ghastly negligee I would no longer be able to enjoy the film. I'd be too concerned by the presence of my mum. 'Christ' I'd think, 'she never mentioned this to me. I won't say anything – she doesn't like me to watch blue movies.' It's a bit like that.

The match at the Boleyn is of little real significance to either side who are both assured mid-table mediocrity this season but for the fans it'll be important. As far as we're concerned our mum's dignity is at stake out there.

I shall spare a thought for dear Frank Lampard who lost his mum this week. Frank is a player who has been unduly harangued internationally and domestically despite being a great midfielder and, by all accounts, a lovely bloke. As Avram Grant pointed out some things are more important than football, like mums.

Girls may turn
my head but my
heart is lost

During the last seven days I have watched more football and had more football-related encounters than at any other time this season. I went to Stamford Bridge for Saturday's visit from Manchester United where I met Ray Wilkins and Chopper Harris and mistakenly attempted to chat up Joe Cole's girlfriend (I didn't recognise her – she's really pretty and when she revealed her identity I had to try and re-package the preceding flirting as harmless chivalry) then on to Upton Park for the Newcastle match.

As I arrived I saw Freddie Ljungberg being tipped into an ambulance, then during the match, for which I was 30 minutes late, I was seated next to the CEO's phenomenal girlfriend – just in time to witness Newcastle's two equalising goals and, most extraordinarily of all, afterwards I was whisked off to meet the legendary Paolo Di Canio. All this and it was Champions League semi-final week, not to mention my childhood hero West Ham striker Tony Cottee's flattering insistence that I introduce his forthcoming greatest goals DVD.

'Forever on the precipice of declarations and tears he converses how he played, with captivating intensity'

Any of these events would be sufficient to fill a column thrice this size and taken together they form a gleaming itinerary of unthinkable intrigue and glamour but even cursory examination will reveal that the inescapable embarrassment that accompanies me through life was present at every turn, like a seagull following Eric Cantona anticipating a tasty morsel of bizarre imagery.

Firstly, Saturday's matches. It was the intention to attend both games on opposite sides of London by promptly leaving Chelsea at the whistle, leaping on to a motorbike taxi – like an assassin – and zipping to east London in time for three o'clock. These motorbike taxis did not show up, instead I travelled to the games in a … taxi.

On Fulham Road once disgorged I walked incognito among the Chelsea fans, thinking myself so smart – 'I'm like Henry V, amidst his troops or Luke Skywalker when he dressed as a Stormtrooper, these blue berks have no idea that I, a Hammer, as fiercely opposed to their posh, Osgood doctrine as it's possible to be, am ghosting imperceptibly in their ranks.'

'I'LL PICK YOU UP AT ONE THIRTY, RUSSELL!' bellowed the driver.

The blue flag anthem stammered into silence, the shuffling battalion ceased marching, a police horse exhaled and eyes turned. 'It's Russell Brand' spat the chief of the Headhunters. I steeled myself for the onslaught. 'I'll go down fighting' I pledged. 'You can take my life but you'll never take my freedom,' I screamed as one by one polite adolescents posed at my side for harmless photos.

I saw a beautiful woman sashaying through the throng – my chance for escape; I darted after her regurgitating clichés till she elegantly revealed she was betrothed to England's most naturally gifted player, Joe Cole. Once in the executive lounge I navigated the Wilkins encounter flawlessly – except for badgering him to give me inside information on the Avram Grant situation, he agreed that the problem was succeeding 'the most charismatic man in sport, let alone football'.

Travelling by car meant that it was necessary to leave this scintillating match at half-time – listening to the radio en route I learned of two goals and several enthralling incidents at the Bridge and two home goals at Upton Park. Of course I was in my seat in time to see Obafemi Martins score for the Geordies then moments later Geremi drew them level, confirming my status as a jinxed talisman. My companion for the second half was the heartbreakingly attractive girlfriend of a West Ham executive who I chatted to innocuously whilst the fans behind us hollered 'Oi, focus on the game' and 'Brand! Put her down.'

Matt Johnstone

At full-time I was approached by a club official who informed me that Di Canio was present and had asked to meet me. Through the vestibules and corridors I sweated and fretted the anxious journey that would lead to an audience with an icon. In the flesh, though flesh seems inaccurate as he is all sinew, muscle and passion, Di Canio is a force. Forever on the precipice of declarations and tears he converses how he played with captivating intensity and awesome commitment. He spoke of West Ham with such love and respect that I quite forgot myself.

At one point I touched his shoulder with my hand and it was as if it were connected to the Earth's core, such was the throb of innate potency. He referred to me and West Ham as 'You', e.g. 'You are a great club, you deserve the best' and when he looked into my eyes it was as touching and as visceral as his volley against Chelsea or when he caught the ball to allow Everton keeper Paul Gerrard to receive treatment rather than score. The feelings were all too powerful.

'He's so passionate,' I thought, I wanted to join in, 'I'm going to say something passionate.' After the umpteenth agonisingly sincere handshake I blurted 'I want to thank you for all you gave to this club.' I nearly wept. 'No. Thank you,' retorted Paolo, far more at ease with this manner of discourse. When he departed I reflected with some relief that no one who saw me watching Di Canio leave the room could ever seriously think I'd be interested in their girlfriend, my heart belongs to Di Canio.

Enthralled by a
giddy mist of
climactic
hysteria

It's the last day of term. School's out. It's the final day, *la finale grande* as they say in Euro Disneyland Paris. We think it's all over – it nearly bloody well is. 'Can we bring in toys and forego uniforms?' – 'No, that doesn't really apply here.'

Ah, the lunacy of the season's climax, the excitement, the suspense, the drama – is there anything quite like it? No. *The Apprentice*? Well, yes, maybe. This season it's more enthralling than usual as there is much to be decided, either Manchester United or Chelsea could be crowned champions this weekend and two from Bolton, Fulham, Reading and Birmingham could be relegated – though Bolton would be remarkably unlucky and, as at the top, their demotion would be due to 'goal difference'.

Perhaps it's this elevation of minutiae, goals conceded and scored potentially deciding the future of fans and players and managers that has produced this giggly mist of climactic hysteria that appears to be affecting everyone from super-agent Pini Zahavi to Manchester City owner Thaksin Shinawatra.

'I've never been one for the ol' prejudice, thinking it a pointless restriction on potential sexual partners'

Shinawatra has sacked Sven-Goran Eriksson, more beloved to the people of Manchester than Noel Gallagher or LS Lowry, on the flimsy basis that City didn't qualify for the Champions League. The Champions League only has a limited number of places; these barmy (human-rights abusing?) magnates from around the globe are at some stage going to have to acknowledge that fact. Unless it becomes simply a league in which any team can participate, with mixed gender sides that have scarcely played before or even met, there will always be some tycoons who finish the season empty-handed.

My mates who are City fans are right browned off about Sven's sacking; in fact it's taken this for them to register even a smithereen of disdain for Thaksin. 'He may be an abuser of human rights you know,' I'd say. 'Who cares? We've got Elano,' came the reply. 'Here, he's sacked Sven ...' 'What?!?!?!?! Someone call Geneva – you can't treat people like that.'

Zahavi has piped up on the topic of human rights claiming that the antipathy towards his client Avram Grant could be rooted in antisemitism. Hmm, I hope not, I always thought it was because he had replaced the world's most twinkly, sparkly, arseachingly attractive Rat-Pack refugee José Mourinho. I don't think his religion is a factor, personally when I learned of his Holocaust day pilgrimage and the murder of some of his family at the hands of the Nazis it made me like him more but then I've never been one for the ol' prejudice, thinking it a pointless restriction on potential sexual partners.

Not that Avram Grant was ever in my sights as a lover nor am I suggesting that he'd have me – he seems very happy with his wife, who, as we all know, drinks wee-wee, a boon for any marriage. Mourinho on the other hand? Why, I'd follow him across the globe as diligently as Didier Drogba for just a whiff off his neck. Drogba incidentally takes second place in my ill-advised Russell Brand Glasshouses Award for Rubbish

David Humphries

Haircuts, behind Arsenal's Emmanuel Adebayor who wins because his shift from corn rows to box top as well as looking less cool coincided with a dip in form and almost total cessation in scoring whereas Drogba's 'do' just looks daft. I know, I know – that's why it's called the Glasshouses Award.

Will Chelsea's fans take to Grant even if he completes an unlikely double? Will they sing his name? Alan Curbishley doesn't get his name sung at Upton Park – he too replaced a manager who was popular with fans, Alan Pardew, who, by no stretch of the most elastic and LSD-doused imaginations, is a match for José Mourinho.

It can't be much fun not to feel loved by your crowd. Now hang on to your hats because I'm about to drop a name so heavy you might piddle yourself with envy – here goes … Jimmy Tarbuck once said to me: 'They like ya kid, and that goes a long way.' He cited the example of the lovely Bob Monkhouse who he said was a brilliant comic and a lovely man but who didn't have the same rapport with an audience as Eric Morecambe or Tommy Cooper. He went to great lengths to point out that Monkhouse was great and delightful but needed to work to get an audience onside.

I suppose this is Grant's dilemma but then Sven was no Sammy Davis Jr and the Eastland's faithful are holding a march to protest his departure, because he got results. In 48 hours it'll all be over, heroes will rise and fall but the game goes on. Adulation, to a point, can be earned but for some it'll be gifted – look at Kevin Keegan, while we still can.

United to win - the
Gods'll never work
this one out

I feel bound to mention that I am writing this article on a flight from New York to Los Angeles having just been on the Letterman show. I bring this up because there is currently turbulence and it might be my fault as I left this laptop turned on, ignoring the announcement: 'All electrical items must be turned off,' which I've always assumed to be a needless imposition of authority rather than an aviational necessity.

'It may interfere with the instruments' – yes, well, it may not interfere with the instruments; then I'd look rather foolish, groping around in those inexplicably lofty cupboards trying to switch it off – all nervous like a Nan or Dennis Bergkamp. Assuming you're reading this all must be well; unless my laptop has been plucked from the wreckage along with the black box – 'Are there any survivors?' 'Never mind that, there's Russell Brand's smoking computer – just pray he had time to save his *Guardian* column. Thank God – then all was not lost.'

'Giggs's record would not be more stupendously commendable if he'd won more wars than Churchill'

In that morbid spirit I shall make some teary predictions for the season's climactic fixtures – bear in mind of course that when making predictions one must consider the possible negative influence of the prediction itself. For example, if I predict that West Ham will win the league next season this will infuriate the Gods, who will punish me by condemning West Ham to relegation, thus I must trick the Gods by predicting outcomes that would displease me. However the Gods are not stupid, they are, after all, omnipotent deities, so I can't just predict the opposite of what I want – the Gods'll see through that in an instant, so I'll mix it up a bit.

First the FA Cup. I believe the Hammers were the last club outside the top flight to win this tournament (in 1980 against Arsenal) an honour I would hate to see overturned by Cardiff, particularly as I recall with fury a visit to the Millennium Stadium where the home support taunted the Claret and Blue Army with an a capella version of the *Steptoe and Son* theme tune 'Old Ned' which was bizarrely sarcastic and demeaning and West Ham capitulated; I think out of a Harold Steptoe-style sense of inadequacy and the futility of trying to improve. Also Harry Redknapp leads Pompey and I love him and consider him to be the last representative of the 'speak yer mind'-type English football managers. So … I predict Cardiff will win.

The Champions League final is interesting. It would be nice for Avram Grant to get some recognition or alternatively to see what means people would employ to continue to deny him credit in the face of such an awesome triumph – 'The players won it themselves' or 'It was a fix' or even 'Abramovich released spores into the stadium whilst fertilising eggs his wife had lain under the pitch which rendered the United players impotent with maternal envy.'

Victory for the Red Devils would bring Fergie closer to his ultimate, recently revealed aim of surpassing the achievements of Liverpool. I think it was Roy Keane who let this info slip and it makes sense to me. I think Sir Alex is one of the greatest living Britons and to fulfil this objective he'd need at least two more seasons as United's manager.

I enjoyed seeing Ryan Giggs equalling Bobby Charlton's appearance record as it gave me a sense of living through history; Bobby Charlton is an evocative figure and his name is so laden with significance that Giggs's record would not be more stupendously commendable if he'd won more wars than Churchill or been more serene than Ghandi. In this instance then, I predict United will win. Them Gods'll ne'er unravel this code – it'd baffle Dan Brown with its complexity.

Finally the Championship play-offs. Hull City versus Bristol City. I've a very dear friend, Gareth, who supports Hull; I feel a deep fondness for folk who follow unglamorous clubs – West Ham, even when relegated, retain a sense of Cockney pizzazz, barra boy razzmatazz, but Hull? I am not speaking out of blind prejudice, I went there once to do a gig and I saw

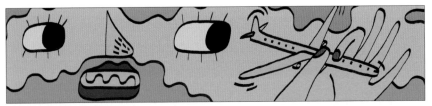

Matthewthehorse.co.uk

three separate brawls in the street. These outbursts of unrest were not I assure you related to my performance nor the floods that at that time blighted the city. Locals informed me it was simply the high-spirited horseplay that accompanies every Friday night's last-orders bell.

When my mates and I discuss football – we all follow Premier League clubs with rich histories, The Irons, United, Liverpool, even Spurs – Gareth must meekly proffer a titbit on Dean Windass or a trip to Palace. I'd love Hull to be next season's Derby; the biggest win I ever saw was West Ham 7 Hull City 1. To which end I hope the Tigers overcome Bristol but predict the reverse. I must go, this turbulence is becoming unbearable and a sky marshal is threatening to have me interned. Even Nostradamus couldn't've predicted that.

One little slip and
happiness goes out
the window

'On what little things does happiness depend!' wrote Oscar Wilde in *The Nightingale and the Rose*. He was referring to the heartbreak endured by a student who needed to get a red rose to impress a professor's daughter. Actually it turned out that the professor's daughter was a bloody idiot and didn't deserve the red rose that was only secured through the agonising death of a lovely nightingale; he should've just written a request for fellatio on the back of a bus ticket and stuck it to her forehead – and insisted on the return of the ticket.

For the want of little things like three titchy little points and John Terry's balance Chelsea's season has expired without glory. It seems ridiculous that the difference between historic triumph and aching disappointment was a wet pitch and a penalty slip from JT, as sure-footed a man as has ever pulled on a boot. Once it becomes a spot-kick showdown irrationality takes hold and on Wednesday I think this was more in evidence than usual; playing in Moscow on a flown-in pitch at 1am after 120 minutes of football and Didier Drogba's green mile strut out of the English game in the pouring rain, no wonder the players were tired and confused.

'Sad that Drogba should depart under a cloud – the last action stains the retina and informs the legacy'

Sad that Drogba who, diving and whining aside, has graced the Premier League with such excellence should depart under a cloud for a feeble slap. Events like that linger – Zinedine Zidane was one of the modern game's finest practitioners yet it is now impossible to think of him without recalling his World Cup final headbutt and subsequent sending off. The last action stains the retina and informs the legacy.

Were I to stage an impeccable concert, an hour and a half of ribticklers and humdingers then, after my ovation, as I left the stage jauntily kick the

Adrian Johnson

choice lady right up the privates those in attendance would unlikely recall the well-structured anecdotes that led to the physical assault, the gig would become known as the fanny-kick night.

If the Queen on her death bed darts onto the balcony at Buckingham Palace and piddles onto the assembled press below people will no longer talk of the death of Diana as her darkest hour, they will say 'the Queen let herself down there, with the ol' death bed micturation fiasco' and rightly so.

Cristiano Ronaldo is lucky that his penalty miss was rendered irrelevant by United's victory, otherwise the season where he has metamorphosed into the world's greatest footballer would become known as a cock-up. Manchester United will not be queried when people look at the record books, how close they came to finishing the season without a bean will not be recollected; they are champions of Europe and England and Sir Alex moves closer to the summit of sporting achievement.

How Avram Grant will be remembered still seems a little less clear. Abramovich was present for his side's narrow defeat and typically you would imagine that a squad that came so close to success would be applauded and nurtured but I imagine in this case that the players will scatter around the globe and that Grant will quietly shuffle off into a den of bureaucracy – which will suit him all the better, he never looked happy on that touch-line.

The incident that for me was emblematic of his reign came in the second leg of the Champions League semi-final when he attempted to retrieve a ball that had rolled towards the dug-out and was battered on to his arse by Steven Gerrard who was undertaking the same act of retrieval with considerably more gusto. It was a bit sad. He looked a bit like a mugged geriatric sat there all confused. The other folk on the Chelsea bench offered no chastisement of Gerrard and no comfort to Grant but just stared ahead and he was forced to do the same but you could see he was all shook up by the encounter and that his heart would've been racing.

The triumphs of Sir Alex Ferguson will be what define this past season but numerous other sub-plots will linger in the mind, among them Grant's doomed stewardship, Liverpool's failure to make a title challenge in spite of the acquisition of a truly great striker in Fernando Torres and the return of Kevin Keegan.

A troubling contradiction for English football comes in the form of our dominance of the Champions League and our inability to qualify for the European Championship – it's a bit gloomy that after this astonishing campaign we must now endure a major international tournament in which we shan't be represented. By mid July I will've forgotten the sense of superiority that I had in May and will be consumed once more with post-colonial doubt.

With no home nation to root for I might yield to xenophobia, yelping at the jinxing foreigners that dart across my screen, blaming them for depriving Englishmen of top-flight football with their talent and their diets. But the truth is 10 English blokes contested that match on Wednesday and this season has shown Sven-Goran Eriksson to be a brilliant manager, unjustly sacked. Football does not make sense.

THE SMASH HIT TV SHOW ON DVD NOVEMBER 08

RUSSELL BRAND'S
PONDERLAND

INCLUDES UNSEEN STAND-UP PERFORMANCES

UNIVERSAL

© 2008 Universal Studios. All Rights Reserved.